A Survival Guide to the End Times

Also by William Wildblood

Meeting the Masters
978-1-78099-168-9 (Paperback)
978-1-78099-169-6 (ebook)

Remember the Creator
978-1-78535-927-9 (Paperback)
978-1-78535-928-6 (ebook)

Earth is a School
978-1-78904-791-2 (Paperback)
978-1-78904-792-9 (ebook)

By No Means Equal
978-1-80341-348-8 (Paperback)
978-1-80341-3489-5 (ebook)

What People Are Saying About

A Survival Guide to the End Times

In End Times, spirit withdraws from the world leaving a physical corpse. Many rejoice over this inanimation because they believe progress exorcises spirit, a phantom in any case. Their rejoicing is part of End Times because this is a great winnowing of souls. William Wildblood writes as a Johannine Christian, so his End Times is not merely a wasting Götterdämmerung or a decomposing Kali Yuga. It is a test that divides men and women by their responses to the withdrawal of spirit. Some rejoice and some lament, and some who lament lose faith that the withdrawn spirit was ever real. This book is for those who lament but keep faith, and hope to remain good grain in the great winnowing of souls. It is an excellent and much-needed survival guide for those who have entered the wilderness and hope for more than to leave their dust in this dry and stony place.
Jonathan M. Smith, PhD, Professor, Department of Geography, Texas A&M University, Editor of Philosophy and Geography

There are many signs that these are the End Times; but what does this really mean?
William Wildblood's subtle and nuanced explanations are focused on the underlying spiritual realities behind the more obvious material changes.
He explores many of the necessary implications for our attitudes and behaviours, if we hope to survive this challenging era with integrity and hope.

I have been reading William Wildblood's writings for a decade, and he continues to surprise and challenge me by the depth and originality of his insights.
Bruce G. Charlton, MD, author of *Addicted to Distraction: Psychological Consequences of the Modern Mass Media*

A powerful, thought-provoking, and candid assessment of our current Western cultural state of decline, inner decay, and existential disintegration in terms of Christian end times and the Kali Yuga cycle. The remedy proposed is in terms of inner orientation – a commitment to being in but not of the world as Christ preached, and a recognition of the need for a purging of the old before the new can come into being.
David Lorimer, Global Ambassador & Programme Director of the Scientific and Medical Network, Editor of *Paradigm Explorer*, and Chair of the Galileo Commission

A Survival Guide to the End Times

William Wildblood

MANTRA
BOOKS

London, UK
Washington, DC, USA

CollectiveInk

First published by Mantra Books, 2026
Mantra Books is an imprint of Collective Ink Ltd.,
Unit 11, Shepperton House, 89 Shepperton Road, London, N1 3DF
office@collectiveinkbooks.com
www.collectiveinkbooks.com
www.mantra-books.net

For distributor details and how to order please visit the 'Ordering' section on our website.

ISBN: 978 1 917704 30 4
978 1 917704 41 0 (ebook)
Library of Congress Control Number: 2025906252

A CIP catalogue record for this book is available from the British Library.

Design: Lapiz Digital Services

UK: Printed and bound by CPI Group (UK) Ltd, Croydon, CR0 4YY
Printed in North America by CPI GPS partners

Contents

Introduction

Ever since the beginning of Christianity a group of believers have thought they were living in the end times and prepared accordingly. Basing this belief on the words of Jesus himself and the book of Revelation attributed to St. John, they saw the world around them as lapsing into spiritual decay and human beings as falling away from God into self-concern and atheism. For them this prefigured the return of Christ in glory and the salvation of all those who believed in him.

It never happened. Despite Jesus's words that "this generation shall not pass, till all these things be fulfilled," the end times never came. But this didn't stop many subsequent generations from believing that they too were living at a time of universal decline. Now, we in the 21st century are faced with a similar dilemma. You could think, here we go again. Those believers never learn from their mistakes. How they must love their pessimism and the sense of self-righteousness it gives them.

But something is different today. The signs of spiritual decay are more obvious than ever before with not just atheism and materialism dominating the minds of most people but even spirituality, where it exists, being often just a form of therapy aimed at comforting the lower self rather than enabling one to go beyond it. And then Christianity has spread all over the world, as was predicted must happen before the end times came, but its power has greatly waned, especially in its former heartlands, and Christians themselves are increasingly persecuted, on the one hand, while, on the other, their churches have fallen into a sort of secular humanism, voided of the supernatural element and more concerned with this world than the next. Meanwhile, even many nonreligious people, increasingly since the turn of the millennium, feel that history has run its course and no longer look with optimism towards a brighter future, but see instead one of growing poverty and cultural loss.

This book takes for granted that we are indeed living in the end times though whether these extend for several more years or decades or longer than that is a different question. If even Jesus said that only the Father knows when these things will happen, it makes little sense to speculate. Nor is there any real speculation here as to how the end times may conclude or what comes after. Christians expect the advent of the Antichrist followed by the return of Christ himself, and a more universal tradition sees the conclusion of the current Iron Age in large-scale destruction followed by a new Golden Age. Given that spiritual ideas are often expressed symbolically, these could be pointing towards the same thing which is not to say that Christ is just one more avatar among many, but that pre-Christian and pagan ideas were visions of what became reality with Christ.

Entropy exists in the spiritual sense as well as the physical. At the start of a new cycle spiritual energy is released into the world from above and it forms a new culture which subsequently runs through the normal stages of growth, maturity, decline and death. The initial energy can be renewed at various points in the cycle, rather like saints can revivify religion, but there comes a time when even this possibility has passed. Today we live at a time when spiritual energy has dissipated to such an extent that the power of matter has asserted itself over everything. The physical and natural environments have hardened and coarsened while, on the mental plane, everyone is cut off from the presence of spirit. This affects even believers, which is why saints and miracles are so thin on the ground these days. I do not say that there are no highly evolved souls around. There may, paradoxically enough, be many but they too will suffer from the world conditions which are universal.

In this book we will examine the end times from a variety of perspectives. We will look at their manifestations, some of which are often regarded as positive by those still in thrall to the psychological consequences of the end times inversion of spirit and matter, and consider their significance from the spiritual perspective. We will look at ways in which the soul may separate itself from the downwards pull of end times energy and also examine how greater familiarity with the ideas of tradition might rescue modern people brought up and educated, brainwashed one might say, in modern ways which are ways that derive from the aforementioned inverted ideology of end times energy in which quantity and matter take precedence over quality and spirit. The subject has endless ramifications, and we will only look at a selection of them, but if one bears in mind the basic theme of the end times, that being the dominance of matter over spirit, it becomes easy to recognise it and therefore resist it in almost every walk of life here and now in the 21st century. That way lies freedom because if you submit to the end times energy, notwithstanding the fact that no one can fully escape it, you are a spiritual slave. These days it is necessary to swim against the tide but, in doing so, we develop our spiritual muscles more than we might do in a more convivial age. The end times may be a period of dissolution and decline but they offer a chance to learn virtues not possible in a Golden Age which would, by definition, lack the challenges and difficulties of the present time. You can only put your courage to the test when there is danger. Such is the nature of our troubled age.

The book is laid out in four sections which look at various aspects of spiritual life in the end times. There is a section on tradition because that is what is negated in the name of progress and much of what we think of as progress derives from the destruction of tradition. This doesn't mean we should get back to tradition as it was, but we should have developed it as Jesus did when he said he came to fulfil the law and the prophets and not to abolish them. God wants humanity to evolve which means unfold, and evolution doesn't contradict tradition, or else what is unfolding? It builds on it sometimes even expanding its dimensions, but it never razes it to the ground, still less does it go radically against it as so much does in our time. Therefore, we can say that tradition should not be slavishly adhered to, but it should be known, recognised, and respected, and the wisdom it contains used as a basis for future growth. The flower only develops from the seed.

The end times are here. They cannot be avoided. You cannot hide from them because they are inside you just as much as out there. They are in the desert and on the mountaintops, on remote islands as well as in the bustle of the city. Nonetheless, by understanding the process you can step aside from the current that is sweeping everything in the world to some kind of conclusion. By knowing it for what it is you can even use end times energy against itself and awaken spiritually, just as when evil shows its true face you may better recognise good. Surviving the end times means building an inner defence. Material survival is not the point, but you should construct a safe haven of spiritual understanding within your mind for the preservation of what is truly important which is your own self.

Some of the pieces here may seem to have only a peripheral relationship to the main theme, but they are included deliberately. That is because everything now is affected by end times energy, and even things we take for granted are revealed on closer inspection to be spiritually debased and in need of reassessment. It is important to get right into the roots of this phenomenon, and that entails looking at everything you have been taught and think you know with fresh eyes.

Part One

End Times

A Body of Slag

It is a truism of esoteric thought that our planet has descended from a pure spiritual state to ever denser forms in which matter has hardened or condensed until we have arrived where we are now. This all accompanies, indeed it facilitates, the evolution of consciousness which gradually separates out from unconscious oneness with the whole to a more individual form before returning to the source, but with the fruits of the journey which would include a fully-exercisable freedom and creative ability.

Another way of seeing the process is that the path of spiritual growth involves reascending from matter to spirit, though emerging life must first be brought to the point at which it can do this consciously and of its own volition. This means the descent to matter was part of the evolutionary journey. There would have been times in the distant past when a form of materially focused consciousness was conducive to overall evolution. One can see the process of physical sex as part of that. It anchors one to the physical body. However, those times are long gone and any return to ways justified in the past is atavistic in the extreme.

Now is the time of greatest immersion in matter. It's the nadir of the arc which means reascending is critical, but it is not inevitable. The reascent can take place either individually or collectively. It should take place on both levels but we, as in each one of us, can only control the former. Now is an important phase in the ongoing evolutionary cycle of the Earth. If enough people reject materialism and turn to the divine, we, humanity and the planet as well, can begin to spiritualise ourselves. The environment will respond to that and change, becoming more rarified. On the other hand, if we, or enough of us, do not do that the descent will continue until in the sobering words of the philosopher Jeremy Naydler, *"a 'body of slag' will be cast off from the Earth as the latter transitions to a higher spiritual state."* What this implies is a kind of split in planetary consciousness with those who are open to God ascending in one purified planetary environment while those who cling to their materialistic ways will descend to a denser environment that reflects their own consciousness. It is a parting of the ways. What matters here is not simply a question of good and bad as we consider those qualities now. Selfishness is certainly part of it, but it is also a materialistic attitude to life. Many who see themselves as upright decent citizens will descend if they remain closed to God. Some sinners will rise if they are sincerely open to God.

Think of human life as a stream moving towards a rock. Part of that stream will go to one side of the rock and continue its way to the sea. The other part will go to the other side and enter a crack in the ground from where it will descend to a subterranean lake. The rock is coming into view. We need to start getting ourselves in place so that we do not consign ourselves to the body of slag for note this: nobody or nothing does this to us. Our own consciousness will determine our external environment.

Slag is the waste product that is separated out from metal ore when it is refined. It is a chilling description for human souls that don't make the grade, but while God is love he is not sentimental. The essence of the human condition is that we are free. If we advance a small way towards God, he will come a long way towards us, but we must make the initial approach. If we don't, we cannot be forced. I would not compare the body of slag to hell, though it may be hellish, because I believe that there will be opportunities to rise again even from that state. But it will be harder. Souls that find themselves there will be that much further separated from real goodness and truth. Everything will be heavier, darker, duller. The time is coming when the rejection of God will have profound consequences. A sheep and goats moment awaits us.

There is a saying in the book of Malachi, well known through Handel's use of it in *Messiah,* that God is like a refiner's fire. He is the divine alchemist who uses heat to purify so that the substance subjected to the heat may be transformed. That substance, the raw material on which God works, is us, and the end times is that period when everything starts to get hotter in order to speed up the experiment. To use an analogy suggested by the writer Joscelyn Godwin, imagine the whole Earth as an alchemist's vessel and humanity as the base metal derived from the *prima materia* which is to be transformed into gold. This tells us we are not gold to begin with as some teachings would maintain. We must become so both by the actions of the alchemist and by our own cooperation with those actions. Gold may be potentially in us, like a little spark of secret light hidden deep within the mine of the heart, but it must be brought out and that is a long and arduous process.

The alchemist subjects his material to various experiments at different times. Some of these can be related to historical periods and some to civilisations which grow, flourish and fall while expressing their own particular qualities. But always the material is being developed and refined. In the past the alchemist may have carefully washed this material to clean it from the outside. Now he is trying a different way. He has withdrawn from sight and left the experiment to itself while applying immense pressure and seeking to draw out inner impurities by bringing these to the surface through the action of heat. Because the material on which he works is not passive but conscious and, to an extent, self-determining, this is a risk which could bring success or disaster or even both depending on individual reaction. But what it tells us is that the end times, for all its qualities of dissolution and decline, is a time of opportunity in that the withdrawing of spirit prompts the active search for it.

Space Is Contracting, Time Is Accelerating

I suggest this is a real phenomenon. You may think space has appeared to contract because technology has reduced distance while time seems to rush by because life has become so fast and rapidly changing. I would not dispute that, but I would also maintain that this is more than an impression because of our circumstances. It is really happening as the cosmic environment changes, though it cannot be measured because any instruments we have would be subject to the same forces that are bringing it about. And the reason it is happening is that we are deep in the Kali Yuga or End Times when spirit withdraws from the world and matter becomes more dominant. This means the very stuff of our current world, now old and worn, is less resistant to the forces of decay and entropy. Consciousness, too, is affected becoming more constricted.

The idea of there being four ages in a cycle is well established in religious cosmology. Many traditions speak of this. Egyptian, Indian, and Greek myths all refer to it, and these are only the best known. The ages can be characterised as Gold, Silver, Bronze, and Iron, and in every case, there is a descent from a high spiritual state of being to a low material one. At the beginning, space is vast and time moves extremely slowly. This is why there are the stories of men living for hundreds of years back in prehistory. It is also why change only comes about after great spans of time. There is no proper notion of history since the patterns of life just repeat. Even the idea of a flat earth, while not literally true, gives a greater sense of endless space than the spherical reality with which, by the possibility of returning to where you started, there is a greater feeling of circumscription.

As the ages proceed human relationship to time changes. Everything is cyclical for early man, each new year resembles the one before, but gradually there arises the idea of linear time. The material aspect of the world solidifies and the spiritual moves further away from perception. The process gathers pace until, as the end of the whole cycle approaches, the cosmic framework in which we live reaches such a point of degeneration that it becomes unstable.

This world was originally structured on the pattern of the heavens. What that means is that the eternal realities of the higher worlds of being were the template on which human societies were based. We can see this clearly in the cases of ancient Egypt and India, but it would apply everywhere to the degree that it could, reflecting the quality of human consciousness at a particular period. A basic principle was the idea of a complementary duality which was the source of creation, heaven and earth, spirit and matter and, in biological terms, male and female. In the beginning there is a correct relationship between these two polarities and they function harmoniously, but towards the end of the cycle, due to the widening gulf between higher and lower states of being, this relationship is disrupted and becomes antagonistic. This leads to an inversion of the hierarchy but also attempts to flatten any kind of hierarchy, and then any kind of difference, at all. This is in line with the developing predominance of matter over spirit. When the active and receptive poles of being are functioning according to their proper nature, all is well. But in a decaying environment everything starts to break down, matter seeks to usurp the rights of spirit, and the relationship between the two ceases to operate creatively. The end approaches.

Back in the day advocates of New Age theory looked forward to the world entering the Age of Aquarius when people would experience a so-called quantum leap shift of consciousness. They acknowledged there would be earth changes as the old age crumbled but appeared to think they and many others would be around to enter a glorious New Age once that had occurred without facing death. This was to misunderstand the doctrine of the ages. It is not like winter gently turning into spring and a new year carrying on in the same way. The end of an age is an end. A new beginning is precisely that. It is a fresh start, and the past is cleared away. When a new heaven and a new earth arrive everything that belongs to the old order must die. Perhaps to be reborn if it has oriented itself correctly, but still, it must first go through death. Transformation always requires death.

You might wonder where Jesus Christ comes into this scenario since, as depicted in tradition, it is a universal phenomenon, independent of him. What Christ adds to the teaching of cyclical ages is the idea of a linear progression to the End Times and a new creation. The Kali Yuga and the End Times are not the same, but they have much in common in how they play out. The Kali Yuga even concludes with the incarnation of Kalki, an avatar of Vishnu, who ushers in a new Golden Age or Satya Yuga. However, this is still part of an ongoing cycle which doesn't really have a conclusion except in *Mahapralaya* which is the complete dissolution of the cosmos and return to non-manifestation. What Christ offers is different. It is a new creation, a new heaven and earth. This is not just another Golden Age which will inevitably degenerate. It is a radical restructuring of reality in which evil and suffering, decay and death no longer have any part, and it is open to all those who wish to partake in it with the proviso that they must also restructure themselves in accord with it. This may be impossible in the literal sense, but we can allow ourselves to be restructured by opening ourselves up completely to Christ. This entails not just belief but love.

Christ is the lifeboat that rescues us from the spiritual wreckage of the Kali Yuga. Increasingly, all people who regard themselves as on the spiritual path or who are just looking for answers in these times of universal decline, value inversion, and all-pervasive spread of evil will find they have to turn to him in some form. As time rushes on towards its final destination, this is how we can survive the collapse.

The End Times Is the End of Term

Demographers estimate that 109 billion people have lived on the Earth over the last 192,000 years, that being the date at which humans are seen as becoming properly human in the sense we now understand that designation. If you add to this figure the number of people alive today you get a total of 117 billion humans which means that 7% of people who ever lived are living now. It is thought that around 9 billion lived before the Agricultural Revolution in about 10,000 BC, and that at that time there were around 5 million humans in the world, but since the Industrial Revolution the number has climbed dramatically with the global population hitting 1 billion around 1800 and then shooting up to where we are now. If you consider that up until relatively recently almost half the population died in childhood whereas infant mortality is very low now our present situation seems even more remarkable.

Obviously, the figures before recent times are highly speculative, but they are not based on nothing, and the numbers and general trends they indicate are probably accurate enough to give an idea of the state of the human population. My question is, does this mean anything from the spiritual point of view, from the evolution of the soul's point of view, or is it just a result of technological advances, medicine, agriculture etc.? It certainly is a result of that but is this all there is to it?

My earlier book *Earth is a School* examined the case for this world as a training ground for the soul. Part of the mechanism for this training is reincarnation which involves an infant soul returning to a particular environment to develop its inchoate capacities, mental, moral, creative, and so on. It is also required to make a choice in a world in which that choice can go either way for the reality of God is not a given here as it would be in the spiritual worlds. Here there is just enough material data to support either the acceptance or rejection of God so the inbuilt orientation of the soul, whether it is aligned to God or to self, is brought into play. Predominantly aligned, I mean, for both tendencies are always present in the soul because of free will.

The need for this choice has always been present but what is happening now is that everything is being brought to a head. This is why there is such a large population, and is yet another indication we are in that period known as the End Times. Extending the school analogy, this is the time of graduation. No doubt some souls have already graduated (I personally think only relatively few have done so), but now is the final exam for many with the choices becoming more marked. We live during a period when religion has lost its power so the choice we make is necessarily more of an individual one. It even must go against the flow which makes it more personal and a truer test of our inner self. Those who pass will progress to higher spiritual worlds while those who don't make the grade will have to continue on lower levels of being with, no doubt, fresh opportunities further down the line but they will have missed an important cut-off point.

Let us imagine souls are given the choice of being born in the physical world except, perhaps, for those very young and inexperienced ones who must follow a path laid down for them by their teachers. But once a soul has developed a measure of understanding and some real independence of agency it can decide when to pursue its education in matter. The material world is tough, but it also offers opportunities to advance not available elsewhere precisely because of the easier conditions that prevail in higher spheres of existence. Compare the safety of the womb with the challenges of the external world for an analogy. Now, in these end times of greater separation from the source, there is very little spiritual support. This makes it tougher, but it also gives a soul the chance to make real progress because the lack of outer support obliges you go within to find your own connection to God. All true growth must come from the inside and the end times force that because of their anti-spiritual nature. It would seem reasonable that many souls would wish to avail themselves of the opportunity to make faster progress.

A word of warning though. The same thing that gives the chance for greater progress also provides obstacles to that progress meaning that while some of us may rise higher, others may fall due to their failure to resist the spiritually constrictive qualities of the end times.

The end of an age is many things, and one of these is that it is a time of coming together when strands that have been evolving separately in the past are assembled so that their different qualities may be brought together in the whole. This is why nowhere in the present day is isolated and everything is aware of everything else, to a degree at least. It is why all periods of the past have been opened up to us in the present, and all cultures exposed to all other cultures. This can lead to an unholy mess, greater breadth, less depth, all things become superficial, everything is equal, nothing is better, nothing worse. But there is also the possibility of extracting the inner essence of all past and present manifestations of the human spirit, and forging a humanity made wiser, stronger, and more rounded as a result. This depends on a careful discrimination between quantity and quality which is a problem as the nature of the end times is to put the focus on the former. But the soul is strengthened by being challenged and its nature tested in adversity.

The end of an age sums up the age which is why so many souls are present then. It is a paying of dues and a handing in of papers and, most of all, it is a gift because for those who make the right choices it is a chance to move into a new state of being.

A New Creation

Christians believe that what Christ offers to those who follow him is a New Creation, worth capitalising, I think. This has relevance in the context of a universal spirituality versus Christianity debate which is pertinent in our time when, as has just been stated, everything is being brought together. I have written in previous books about how the teachings and person of Christ go further than any other form of spirituality, including that of the Buddha. This idea of a New Creation gets to the heart of it. The Buddha saw the reality of suffering and showed a way to escape that. The way involved leaving a fallen creation behind. Essentially, it entailed rejecting the goods of creation for entry into the non-created or pre-creation state. We tend to overlook the fact that original Buddhism was a monastic or world-denying religion. This is a valid response to the evils of this world and the demands of the spiritual quest, but it is not the only one or even the best. The best is that offered by Christ in which matter and spirit, or creation and uncreated divine being are joined together to make something new. Here, matter is sanctified rather than rejected. Latter forms of Buddhism approach this idea, but they never fully embrace it. Other spiritual traditions incorporate elements of this approach, but they all have a fundamental drawback. They lack Christ, and it would be my contention that it is only through Christ that one can fully enter the New Creation. I do not doubt he is present in other religions to the extent that they are open to his spirit, but he can never be as fully present as he is in Christianity where he stands revealed as himself.

This difference has never been more important than it is today in the context of the world as it is now. That is because we are in the middle of a battle between good and evil. A general spirituality which seeks to rise above the world will either be neutral in the face of this battle, beyond good and evil as those aiming at spiritual transcendence might put it, or else it will be sucked into evil. In fact, as genuine neutrality is no longer possible, if it ever was, advocates of this approach will increasingly be drawn onto the side of evil. In our time if you don't actively stand against evil, you tacitly support it, and if you do want to stand against evil, you can only really do that by recognising Christ.

Christ is the embodiment of goodness because he manifests the goodness of the Father absolutely. You cannot say that Christ is good as that implies it is something separate from him that comes before him which he has acquired through acknowledging it. Goodness is not so much in him as revealed through him as the manifestation of God, God's face and form. Other forms might approach or echo that, but he is the living template while they derive what goodness they might have from their openness to him. If you understand what the good is, you must see it is centred in Christ and the more distant from him something is, the less of good it has.

The New Creation came into being when Christ defeated the Prince of this World which is what he did through his life and death. This explains why there was no path to it before his time. It didn't exist. That means that any form of spirituality which originated before Christ does not offer a path to it unless that form has, as I say, subsequently opened itself to the spirit of Christ which is certainly possible as that spirit spread throughout the world after the Incarnation. This is a controversial position to take in the modern age because the egalitarian dogma has spread into every area of life including religion. Also, because we in the West reacted to human misinterpretations and distortions of Christianity either by turning to atheism or by seeking spiritual nourishment elsewhere. But go back to Christ himself and the Gospels, particularly that of St. John, and you will discover a spiritual truth that goes beyond all others, one that does not just offer a way out of the material world but purifies that world so rendering it capable of being lifted up into spirit and becoming something new, a new Adam, a new Jerusalem, a new world.

When Jesus spoke of the Kingdom of Heaven, it was this New Creation of which he spoke. Heaven is not just the oneness of undivided spiritual consciousness. It includes that but goes beyond it because it brings to that undifferentiated oneness the qualities and colours of creation. And it brings relationship to oneness which means it brings love. Love existed before Christ's appearance in the world, but it was not fully knowable for humanity until he made it possible for the self, hitherto a centre of egotism from which one could only escape and leave behind, to be holy. No self means no love. Christ made the individual spiritually beautiful and potentially godlike instead of being a disturbance in the still waters of divine oneness. Heaven is full of individuals because it is the abode of love, and this was the New Creation brought by Christ.

Look back into the past and you will see that love as conceived before Christ and love after him are not the same. What changed love and raised it to a higher level was the self-sacrifice of Jesus on the cross. Sacrifice existed in earlier times. It was the basis of most early religions, the Vedic and the Greek, to take just two, but here instead of humanity sacrificing to God we have God sacrificing himself for humanity. This act of love and renunciation opened a channel between the spiritual and material worlds and grounded a higher form of love in the physical where it could be accessed directly by those who gave themselves to Christ, but also indirectly by everyone since it was now present in the planetary psychic atmosphere. The sacrifice of the self in love redeemed the self and sanctified creation. Out of death came transformed life, and the Resurrection and Ascension then brought about the New Creation.

I want to say a word here about what you might call the Nietzschean criticism of Christianity, which is that it is an unmanly religion fit only for a slave mentality as it promotes humility and self-sacrifice while suppressing the individual. There is some justice to this charge, especially in terms of what Christianity became when its supernatural mystery was replaced by a more world-centred morality. However, to understand what Christianity really is you must go back to the figure of Christ himself and see him not only as a saviour but also as an exemplar. Then you see that humility is certainly a Christian virtue, but Christ is still a King, and, in a spiritual sense, I would maintain he is a warrior king. Look at the image on the Shroud of Turin and you should be convinced of that.

So, the self must be sacrificed but there must be a strong self to do this before that operation can be spiritually creative. The experience of Crucifixion, which every soul must pass through before it can enter the Kingdom of Heaven, can only take place after the Transfiguration of the soul on the mountaintop and that can only happen to the fully developed individual, able to withstand the downpouring of spiritual power that is involved at that initiation. The weakness that Nietzsche and others see in Christianity is surely there, but it is not in Christ and our concern is with the Son of God not the faded glories of the religion founded in his name. Everything in this world passes, and in the end times nothing is spared from the ongoing process of dissolution, Christianity included.

The Paths of Peter and John

It could be said that right from the beginning there were two forms of Christianity, that of St. Peter and that of St. John. The former provided an ideal foundation for a public religion with a solid structure for orientating believers towards spiritual truth. That gave a framework for belief in the human and divine figure of Christ, moral instruction and ethical guidance that would lead souls towards salvation which is the regeneration of the soul in the afterlife. This approach emphasised faith and works which together form the two pillars of the doorway that marks the entry to the higher spiritual world. However, following this path still leaves the believer looking for spiritual authority outside himself. He is dependent on externals and remains a follower.

The spiritual approach exemplified by St. John is different. This is the inner approach. Christ remains Christ but he is no longer simply the Son of God who came down from Heaven. He is also within us, within our hearts, and he can be known. More, not only can he be known but we can start to become like him by opening our hearts to his light and truth which will then illuminate our souls and transform them. We will not be human believers in God or followers of Christ but become transformed into spiritual beings ourselves if we allow the soul to be illuminated by the spirit of Christ. He is the light. It might be countered that we are always spiritual beings, and it is true that we were created as such, but we are spiritual beings in embryo only until we develop properly. We are seeds, and seeds must blossom and bloom to fulfil their purpose. And not all seeds do fully blossom.

These two approaches are not mutually exclusive, but they are somewhat like body and soul, and just as in our day there are many people who are aware of themselves as minds and bodies but few who are conscious of themselves as souls, so it is with these approaches. Historically, one can say that the Petrine approach has only occasionally advanced into the Johannine, but humans have evolved to the point at which Christianity can only remain relevant if the Johannine approach becomes known as the direction in which the soul should proceed. It takes the external truths of Christianity and applies them internally.

I am not talking here about the difference between exoteric and esoteric, or hidden teachings revealed only to the initiated. Clearly, there are many things about God and the universe we do not know but what really matters from the spiritual point of view is the orientation of the heart to the good, the beautiful, and the true, and the spiritually perceptive know these are summed up and embodied in Jesus Christ. But there is the Christ 'out there' and the Christ within, and while John includes Peter, Peter does not necessarily include John.

Over the last several centuries humanity has entered the fullness of self-consciousness. This has resulted in two major problems. Because we have developed a stronger sense of our self, we have lost a proper relationship both with what is below the self and what is above it. These are the worlds of nature and spirit which can be thought of as our mother and father. The first we disrespect and exploit, and the second we reject and deny. Consequently, we are in total disharmony with the universe, and this is the root cause of all our problems.

The self has freed itself from that in which it was embedded. This is good because only by doing so can it really begin to know itself, but it becomes bad when the process stops there and congeals. Then barriers are put up against the rest of life, both natural and spiritual. To seek to return to nature in response to this, as some people do when they perceive there is a problem, is wrong because it is a return to childhood and, owing to the developed state of the self, this will be a self-conscious and artificial return. In other words, unnatural. We must go on to a union of the self with spirit and then a proper relationship with the natural will be established but from the higher perspective not on its own terms. However, even the approach to spirit must be the right one. At the time of the decline of the Roman Empire there was great fascination with decayed forms of the ancient mysteries. This was a kind of spiritual sensationalism, indicative of a jaded palate and desire for new experience. The same phenomenon occurs today with many modern versions of mysticism and occultism which are viewed as ways to excite and expand the self, but this is not where true spirituality is to be found. For us in the West that remains where it has been for the last 2000 years, centred in the reality of Christ, only now our approach must be more that of John than of his fellow disciple. Peter is not excluded but to his formal religious approach we need to add the greater depth that is found in John. When Peter asked Jesus what John would do to serve him, he was told that this was no concern of his, but that John would tarry until Jesus came again. This could imply that John's role was beyond Peter's understanding then and would only become comprehensible later when more souls would be able to respond to its deeper spiritual quality. That time is now and so our focus today should be moving from Peter to John so that when Christ does reappear, in whatever form that may be, we are able to recognise him more fully.

The Destruction of the West

To what extent is the current elite deliberately trying to destroy the West, specifically the Christian West, and to what extent is this simply a matter of false ideology and ignorance, short termism and even misplaced good intentions? For, make no mistake, the West is being destroyed, in spirit if not outwardly, though very possibly both. It is being eaten away by materialism, atheism, moral relativism, egalitarianism, and several other movements and ideologies which any rightly oriented person can recognise as maladaptive and spiritually unhealthy. These are often interlinked and result from the loss of the sense of the transcendent on the one hand and the promotion of envy and resentment to virtues on the other. There is usually some perceived good that results from them in some limited area, which is how they get general acceptance, but overall, they are like viruses that infect and incapacitate a healthy body. A virus may seem good on its own terms, but it is not good for its host.

Just as there is a hierarchy of good so there is an inverted hierarchy of evil. At the upper levels of this hierarchy there is intent. Deliberate, serious, cold, malevolent intent. At mid and lower levels, not so much, at least not in the sense of something planned and acknowledged. Some of the people at these levels may want to destroy what they are against more than they want to bring in what they say they are for, but they tell themselves they are motivated by honest impulses to make a better world. And there may be elements of this motivation in their psychological makeup but there are also feelings of anger and hatred. They are co-opted by those at higher levels because of some personal moral defect or intellectual weakness or spiritual vacuum at their core. They may be unwitting servants of evil, but they would not be co-optable if there was not this attraction to sin or spiritual void within them.

But we are all sinners so what's the difference? We all fall short of perfection, and we all have inclinations to selfishness and pursue the goals of the ego at the expense of those of the Good. Very true, we are all sinners, but some people recognise this and struggle against it while others allow themselves to be defined by it. These latter justify, excuse, or even celebrate their sin. They identify with it and do not allow true spiritual feeling to reveal it for what it is. It is their treasure, their pet, rather than their burden; their pride rather than their shame. They will even disguise it to themselves and others as a virtue.

Nothing in this world is 100% one thing. None of us are perfect and none of us are wholly bad. And yet, the world is moving in a direction in which the dividing line between sheep and goats, between those who, on the whole, wish to love and serve God, the truth, the good, however they might define it, and those who, in one way or another, serve the forces of anti-God, anti-truth, anti-good, is being drawn. Tests are underway. These examine our spiritual responses to situations and ideas but be careful of that word spiritual. It does not necessarily mean what we think it does, we who live in a decidedly unspiritual age. Thus, it is not universal loving kindness unless that is balanced with love of real spiritual (as opposed to worldly) good. For instance, everyone would say that God loves us but what does he love? Does he love us as we are, or does he love the soul rather than the earthly personality? Both, you say. Then does he love the murderer as murderer? This is an extreme example, but it illustrates the point that though God loves the sinner, he does not love the sinner as sinner. If the sinner will not let go of his sin he is separating himself from God's love. That will always be there should he repent, and, for the sake of the soul, God will do what he can to bring that sinner to repentance, but he cannot override free will.

Therefore, spiritual response means response to the reality of the world of the soul and to the values of that world. It does not mean treating the lower self as though it were the higher self, but that is often the practice of worldly people, which includes many self-defined religious and spiritual people these days, who lack understanding of that world and who misinterpret the truths of spirit by seeing them in the light of this world and its priorities.

The West is falling, in part by deliberate plan, in part by ignorance, in part by greed, selfishness, and just simple carelessness. But also, because its time has come. If that were not the case, then the attempts to destroy it would not be succeeding as they undoubtedly are. For those who regret its passing, and we should because the death of something that once reached for nobility is tragic, let me quote some words spoken to me many years ago at a time when this process was well underway but had not reached anything like its present state. The words are these and I put them in bold for emphasis. **"Nothing good, nothing true can ever be lost."** When we see how goodness and truth have been abandoned, we are right to lament it, but we should also remember that, however good and true something may have seemed, it was but a pale reflection of what inspired it and that remains inviolate in the higher worlds.

The West is under ferocious attack by the powers of evil. This has been a long-term operation, but it is coming to a head now, and for that reason people who only think in terms of human generations cannot see it for what it is. They think the desire for money or power is what motivates the corrupt elites. But these people are manipulated, their vices exploited, by supernatural powers which seek the separation of the soul from God. Only when you recognise this basic fact can you understand what is going on in the world today. It is natural to mourn the destruction of the good, but it is more important to hold fast to the vision of the divine. Our salvation never lay in this world.

That does not mean we should blithely accept the loss of the good here. We should never do that, but knowing that the real good is elsewhere will give us a proper perspective. In the end times loss is inevitable, which is why one of the most important qualities for survival in these times is detachment.

How to Save the West

Anyone can see that Western civilisation has entered a period of collapse. Let me rephrase that. Anyone should be able to see that Western civilisation has entered a period of collapse, but many people don't because they are too wedded to their own pleasures and desires and ambitions, or simply because they don't want to face reality. Yet, if ever a civilisation deserved to fall, it is ours because we are not worthy of those who established that civilisation. We, who place the temporal above the eternal, put ourselves at the mercy of the temporal and our time has passed.

There is a solution, but we are unlikely to take it. The solution is to return to the soul of Christianity. I do not say to Christianity as the outer religion it was but to its soul which is Christ. That might include a form of what is now dismissed as patriarchy since it is chiefly only men who are willing to fight for truth and to preserve it in the face of the inevitable attacks on it, inevitable because what is described by the term Satan exists and wages an ongoing war against creation. This has become so apparent in our day, and especially over the last 25 years, that anyone who wishes to tread the spiritual path must see that path in terms of the war of good and evil. If you refuse to recognise this, you are being spiritually naive. For in these latter times the mask is coming off and the face of evil beginning to be seen for what it is. These words might seem melodramatic to a cynical modern mindset, but evil is real and must be taken seriously. The Prince of this World is not an idle ruler, loitering in his palace. He is out and about in his domain, prowling around like a roaring lion looking for someone to devour to use the striking image of the apostle Peter.

The powers of evil have attacked the West on many fronts over the last several decades. The attack has been ongoing, but it has been stepped up several degrees because the nature of these times gives greater opportunity. The removal of the protective shield of tradition and the levelling of hierarchical values as Substance starts to dominate Essence, to put it in scholastic terms, strengthen the hand of evil, and so it attacks through many avenues which include the debasement of culture, mass immigration, and feminism.

In a society that recognised and patterned itself on the reality of God and saw its true home as being elsewhere, cultural activity would be directed towards bringing the quality of the higher worlds down to this one. Arts and even crafts would not primarily be means of self-expression but soul expression, and they would endeavour to orient the society upwards. What else is beauty but a reflection of the form of God? A society that has lost touch with God will only seek to express its own shrunken ego through its creative endeavours and will inspire no one. With the celestial path closed off, attention is increasingly dragged down to the infernal which then becomes more revealed and is fed back into the general culture, causing further degradation. Can anyone deny this is our situation today?

In a society that wished to preserve itself foreign immigrants would not be given a say in how the country was run (in other words, a vote) until they had become completely assimilated, and their number would be restricted so they could be assimilated. The number of immigrants that flood into Western countries now will inevitably change those countries beyond recognition. Those committed to certain ideologies might claim the long-term results of that cannot be known, but anyone of sense will know that for a host nation to permit it is borderline insanity because it will become a completely different place thereby. A basic instinct is self-preservation. To go against this instinct is to succumb to the unnatural and the anti-spiritual.

The failure to reproduce and the desire to kill yourself are ungodly. This points to the fact, important to acknowledge, that allowing immigration on the scale that is currently taking place is a sign of national decline and loss of centre before it becomes a contributory cause of it.

Feminism is the devil's secret weapon because, while ostensibly based on reason and justice, it seeks to reverse natural hierarchies and turn the two sexes, meant to be complementary, into rivals on the same ground. The promotion of women to previously male spheres damages society because establishing consensus becomes more important than the search for truth and excellence. Sir John Glubb in his book *The Fate of Empires* remarks that an increase in the influence of women in public life has often been associated with national decline and gives examples from Rome and medieval Baghdad. That having been said, as with immigration, feminism is not the initial cause of the collapse but a symptom of it though it does hurry it along as well.

I say a remedy might be a return to some sort of modified patriarchy meaning one that takes account of the evolution of consciousness and the natural obligations and responsibilities of men and women to each other, but I am not recommending this even if it were possible. Modern men do not acknowledge God. They are in thrall to the material world and their own selves, and therefore they are not capable of sustaining a properly functioning patriarchy, i.e. one that works for both men and women, as that must be founded on the recognition of a higher authority. But even if that were not the case, the West must go the way of earlier civilisations because the creative energies that drove and sustained it have grown feeble, and it has come to the end of its useful life. It is turning into a decaying body on which parasites feed as it dies, but in the greater scheme of things that is not as desperate as it might sound because everything in this world primarily exists to serve spiritual needs. As the West collapses there are spiritual opportunities for those who know how to take advantage of them. We may regret the collapse because of past good but everything dies, and the West has rejected God so become rotten. There is no more to be said. Its time has passed but the good that was in it remains and will be taken up into the spiritual consciousness of humanity.

What Is the Solution to the Current Crisis?

Many people recognise that we live at a time of crisis. We might call it by different names and have varying degrees of insight into the depth of our present predicament, but any thinking person knows we are in trouble. Talk about the massive amount of government and private debt, about societal breakdown or environmental degradation, or about the complete loss of direction of all Western societies. All these are indicative of some sort of crisis, but they are just the outer signs of a deeper malaise. Anyone drawn to a book such as this will know that the true crisis is spiritual, but even those who don't acknowledge that should perceive that something is amiss and badly so.

So, what's the solution?

There is no solution. The last chapter mentioned a return to the soul of Christianity as a potential remedy to the decline, but realistically the nature of the end times precludes that possibility. There is no solution and those who look for one will be disappointed. Those who try to enforce one as in the proposed remedies to the presumed climate crisis will only increase the chaos and confusion. There is no solution because we live at the end of an age or cycle, which means we are in a phase of universal decline and increasing disorder. To say this is not to be pessimistic or negative. It's just a fact. The world goes through cycles which follow the natural pattern of spring, summer, autumn, and winter. To recognise we are deep in winter is simply to see the truth. To seek a solution to that is like an old person seeking to be young again and, not coincidentally, that is something we often do see nowadays. In the case of modern man there is a mass falling away from spiritual belief which leads to materialism and atheism to begin with, and then in some cases as a reaction to that to various false spiritualities. This is the way the world goes when the initial burst of spiritual energy behind the forces that set it in motion starts to fade away and humans try to make their own reality from very limited resources.

We are in the Kali Yuga or End Times which were predicted and were predictable because the tendencies to decline, loss, and value inversion are typical of matter replacing spirit as the predominating force, that being a basic definition of the Kali Yuga. The idea of Kali Yuga may be Indian and that of End Times Christian, and one is cyclical while the other is part of a linear progression, but both say similar things about the nature of the world and the historical process. They come at the phenomenon from different places and describe it from culturally specific points of view but the same insight into the waxing and waning impact of spiritual energy on matter over a certain period is expressed.

The course of human unfoldment follows a cyclical pattern because it is bound to forces that derive from above the material plane which act in the world according to certain rhythms that we can associate with the movement of the stars and planets. The beginning of a cycle sees the introduction of spirit into the world system. This produces the mythological Golden Age when gods walk with men, and the veil between the mortal and celestial worlds is thin. It determines the path to be followed during the next however many millennia the cycle endures (around 26, some believe, based on the 25,800-year precession cycle), but over time its force decreases, though the frameworks it has built remain and can even be developed. Eventually, however, material conditions start to overwhelm the residue of spiritual energy, and then the former begin to dominate. From the human perspective, there is no solution to this other than to build an inner ark, and that is the test of these times. To maintain faith in a world which has either lost it or corrupted it. But this is how the wheat is sorted out from the chaff which you may find an objectionable metaphor given its implications, but John the Baptist used it so it has an authoritative precedent.

This world was designed to develop consciousness, and though it may have deteriorated from its original pure state due to the negative impact of human thought, it still has that function. At certain times it also serves to test the soul, and this is one of those times. The test now is for the soul to acknowledge and turn to God as its Creator, but also to recognise evil as that which opposes God and his purpose for creation. It is not enough simply to believe in God if you are not on his side. That just means the God you choose to believe in is one of your own imaginings, which is the case for many. Humanity has reached a point at which it must make a conscious choice to align itself with God, and the nature of the world today is that this must take place on an individual level. In the past we operated collectively because the culture inclined us in a certain direction but now the culture is in the service of anti-God forces, and we must stand against that if we are to succeed spiritually.

Don't be misled by people who say that a spiritual person has above all else to be a good person. That may be true but good by what criteria? First and foremost, we must recognise what spiritual good is and consciously align ourselves with that. It is the full acknowledgement of God. Obviously, we should try to behave in the way that befits a lover of truth. Faith alone is not an excuse for bad behaviour or a justification for antinomianism. If you love me, keep my commandments. If you don't keep the commandments, you surely do not love he who gave them. Besides which, proper recognition of God will automatically incline a person to seek to be like him. But to be good as the world sees good is not the same thing. Moreover, we all fall short. That does not matter if we try at every moment of the day to *'walk humbly with God'*, to paraphrase the simple but powerful words of the prophet Micah.

There is no outer solution but there is an inner solution. Know yourself to be a soul born in the world at this time to prove you can turn your spiritual compass to true north in a world in which all outer influences run counter to that. Not south, materialism, and atheism, not east nor west, following an outer religion while your heart is still bound to the world, and not even northeast or northwest taking these to mean false forms of spirituality. You must find the way to God within yourself and that is the case even if you follow an established form of religion for that is no longer sufficient on its own and can even be a diversion from the true inner path. Now, there must be a real inner connection, and when you have attained that you simply follow where you are led, wherever that may be.

Saving the West

There are numerous people these days talking about the downfall of the West, and blaming the usual suspects of mass immigration, liberalism, and materialism, and their by-products of sentimentality, self-hatred and so on. We have already discussed these, what are at the same time, symptoms, and causes. Some regret the deepening twilight of our civilisation but accept it as inevitable, others want to fight it and think it can be turned around, while a few just shrug their shoulders and cultivate their garden which seems to them to be the only sensible option left in a crumbling cultural wasteland. I sympathise with all these approaches but would like to ask a question here. What is the West for? Because only if we know what it is for can we know if it is worth saving.

Any civilisation worth that name must be organised around spiritual principles. From ancient Egypt to Greece to India, and Rome too when it began, God or the gods were at the centre of life, formed the culture, and gave meaning to the civilisation. For the West that organising principle was Christianity which was the greatest expression of spiritual understanding there has been. All other expressions, though valid on their own terms, might be said to be from the outside looking in. Only Christianity really comes from the inside. That, of course, is the meaning of revelation, and Christ is the greatest revelation from the spiritual world. There really is no doubt about this. He is the only religious personality utterly without flaw or limitation.

The West existed for the expression of Christianity. That is what gave it its greatness. Not uniquely for there were several pre-existing streams which brought their own distinctive qualities, the spirit of the North and that of the Mediterranean to name two principals, but the river into which these streams flowed was Christian. Some people think the West is defined by science and has reached its greatest state following that pursuit but even science arose in a Christian context with natural philosophers seeking to understand God's creation. And whether it has reached its apogee pursuing science or sunk to a spiritual nadir is a question worth pondering.

When the West started to abandon Christianity, it lost sight of itself. Now, we can go into the reasons for that abandonment and say that some of them were based in truth because they were to do with the development of consciousness and an increased mental polarisation which led to a new comprehension of the creation. The outer expression of Christ's teachings followed by the West might be said to have been suitable for an earlier phase of consciousness, less so for the new phase. But the core remained eternally valid for the core is Christ himself. It is not true that a better grasp of the world leads to atheism. A superficial understanding may but not a deeper one. A little knowledge has proved to be a dangerous thing for the West, but it is not only this superficial knowledge that has caused the West to abandon God and Christ. This is fundamentally a moral problem. The creature has got too big for its boots. Its newly acquired powers have gone to its head for it has taken these to itself and decided they are aspects of its own self and belong to that self by right.

Naturally, as one born and raised in the West, I regret its demise, but it has brought this on itself through its own hubris. When it rejected Christ, it signed its own death warrant, and we live in the playing out of that process. I suppose that it could theoretically rediscover Christ but that looks very unlikely, so much have we succumbed to our own egotism and proved unable to resist the demonic influences which hasten the process of our downfall. Individually, we can and should turn back to reality which means for the West to Christ, but collectively things do not look promising. So be it. The West is only worth saving if it rededicates itself to Christ. Note I do not say spirituality, which can mean a whole host of things, some positive, some just self-indulgent and shallow. Without the rediscovery of Christ, we can fight the symptoms and secondary causes of decline as listed above all we like, but it will not lead to any kind of true renaissance.

Towards the end of the 18th century two cultural phenomena arose which were exclusive to Western consciousness, being linked to its unique qualities of individualism and the need for freedom. These were revolution with its overturning of traditional hierarchies and promotion of new forms of human relationship, and romanticism. Both are powerfully expressed in the music of Beethoven which was a radically different approach to art. It's hard for us to appreciate how different since we are so used to it, but you can get an idea if you listen to composers such as Palestrina, Monteverdi, Bach and Haydn for a while, one after the other, and then come to Beethoven. There is certainly change and development from the 16th to the 18th century, but then there is an explosion. And yet Beethoven only expressed what was current. He gave voice to it, but it was there. It was a new type of consciousness which sought outer change through revolution and inner change through romanticism which was the desire to go beyond current religious structures and experience the divine inwardly. And a greater sense of individuality was the key to everything.

This was a great opportunity. If the new consciousness could have been harnessed to the reality of Christ there might have been a spiritual leap forward. Unfortunately, the revolutionary spirit was captured by the negative forces of anger and hatred, and lost itself in bloodshed, disorder, and chaos, while the romantic spirit rejected the guidance and directing force of proper religion and indulged itself in feelings. Human weakness overcame the downpouring of spiritual energy and set us off on the path we have followed only too faithfully ever since.

If the West had responded to the new impulses that played on it from above by submitting them to the overlordship of Christ it is possible that the influence of the end times could have been mitigated or delayed. The West might have saved itself. On the other hand, this may have only been a temporary reprieve. End times energy would still have been active, and the trend to dissolution would not have gone away. The spirit of romanticism has certainly illumined many minds for the good, but it has had a negative impact as well for it has encouraged narcissism and the seeking out of experience for its own sake. Thrills and personal inflation became more important than genuine spiritual upliftment, and this too may be blamed in part on the forces of materialisation associated with the end times.

World War Two and Its Aftermath

Seeing the path the world has taken over the last 80 years one might wonder whether the demonic forces behind World War Two were not so much aiming to win a conventional victory as hoping to use the reaction against the defeated Nazis to promote their agenda to bring down Western civilisation and, more to the point since that was already on the turn, corrupt human souls.

This is not to say the Nazis weren't the tools of darkness, but might one suggest, without being accused of contrarian revisionism, that they were not uniquely evil either? They, and especially Hitler, have been made into figures of archetypal wickedness, devils in human form, and it suits our self-image to cast them in that light because it makes us appear virtuous, but this is a problem because investing them with such unique evil gives the impression that everything they believed must have been wrong. Consequently, it becomes easy to define good as the opposite of that. This false idea then provides a fruitful area for exploitation in that morality becomes anything that is anti-Nazi.

Let's see how this plays out. The Nazis believed in Aryan supremacy so whatever works against that is good. Anti-racism, mass immigration, belittling one's own people, culture, and country to the point that you accept or even welcome their disappearance if you are an Aryan, i.e. white, all this is good because it is the opposite of what the Nazis believed. If it's good we go along with it even if it is against our own interests and our better judgment. The feeling we should do what is right for some and the glow of moral superiority for others overcome any lingering instincts of self-preservation. You might think this is neutral from a spiritual point of view or even good because of the instruction to love your neighbour, but some of your real neighbours are harmed by the policies that arise from this, both economically and culturally, and no spiritual purpose is served by eroding national cohesion which is what happens when communities with different interests battle for power. More seriously, there are those who see mass immigration and anti-racism as preliminary measures in the construction of a globalist, one world state that would serve as the stage for the Antichrist which would make them far from being spiritually neutral. They may, in fact, be part of an attempt to bring about a kind of spiritual slavery. Let's not beat about the bush. That is the underlying purpose behind them even if this purpose is not realised by the middle-ranking minions who enact it.

The Nazis were against sexual deviance, notwithstanding the personal behaviour of some of them. Therefore, it becomes obvious that sexual liberation is a good thing. To oppose that is to be a cruel fascist, a control freak, a prude, a Nazi. To want to restrict love, you must be a hateful person. Love, or what is called love, is a justification for anything. (By the way, a lot of misunderstandings could be avoided if we, like the ancient Greeks, had more than one word for the many different feelings covered by the simple word 'love'.) But spiritual teachings of every tradition are clear. The sexual energy is the most powerful force we know of, and it must be tamed and channelled correctly if we are to awaken spiritually. Love must be pure to be aligned with the Will of God, and that means expressed according to the energies of creation.

The Nazis wished to ban degenerate art, *Entartete Kunst*, which we know simply as modern art. They saw this as un-German in inspiration and effect, criticising it for its "Freemasonic, Jewish or Communist nature" (Wikipedia). Their defeat left anyone with similar doubts about this kind of art, that it did not reflect the higher worlds as art traditionally was supposed to do but was more in tune with infernal regions, in a difficult position. If the Nazis thought modern art bad, then it must be good. If you too think it's bad, well then, you are a Nazi sympathiser. At the very least, you belong to an outmoded, out of touch, and ignorant group.

And so on. Now, to stop any latent Nazi tendencies to rise up once again we must encourage all those things they were against. Evil then spreads not by force of arms but through propaganda and even morality. And this, I would say, is because we have allowed ourselves to see the war against the Nazis as an absolute good against absolute evil situation. As a result, for the last 80 years World War Two has become a replacement foundation myth for Western civilisation. And yet it was just a war like many others. We need to put it behind us and no longer define ourselves in terms of our reaction to it, but it seems more important now than it ever was. When I was growing up in the 1960s it did not form a major part of my history lessons, but my children's history syllabus seemed to revolve almost entirely around it. They were taught a lot about Hitler and the Holocaust, and practically nothing about Alfred the Great and the Armada.

Maybe the reaction against the Nazi beliefs became Plan B for the dark forces but, in terms of defeating the Christian West, that plan has been most effective. And speaking of Christianity, one should note that this was the one thing the Nazis were against that has not benefitted from an anti-Nazi reactionary support. Coincidence?

The defeat of Germany prompted the emigration of many European Marxists to America where they spread their ideological poison, first in academia and then throughout the culture, in the process capturing all the institutions which now work against the nations they were set up to support. Whether this was part of the plan to begin with or whether it became the plan after military defeat is irrelevant at this point. The fact is the West allowed itself to be infected by a spiritual virus which has caused the sicknesses we suffer from today. Along with

Russia, the West may have won the war on the battlefield, but in that victory, there lay the seeds for its subsequent defeat.

These thoughts on the aftermath of the war are not written as part of a recent trend reassessing the motivations and legacy of Winston Churchill. Churchill was clearly a complicated character. A friend of mine, Michael Lord (see my book *Meeting the Masters*), knew him quite well in his later life and would sometimes be invited to lunch at his house at Chartwell. On one occasion he watched as Churchill fed his pet goose pâté de foie gras from the dinner table, making the bird, in effect, a cannibal. A jolly joke. But, though one might wonder whether the state of Europe after the war was any better than it would have been without a war, with Britain ruined and Eastern Europe communist, it must have seemed at the time as though there was no other option in the face of Nazi aggression, and Churchill was probably the right man to lead the country at that time. However, one may still be permitted to speculate as to whether the dark forces saw the war and its aftermath as a means to infect the West with atheistic communism as it had to that point proved reasonably resistant to that spiritual disease, a disease to which we have now succumbed if you look at it, as you should, as something much more than an economic system.

There are many people now pointing to the, to all intents and purposes, communist takeover of the West and how we are being taught by this ideology to hate ourselves and our past achievements. Our countries are being filled with aliens and our cultures debased. The family, which is the bedrock of a stable society, is undermined, and hierarchical structures, which, properly understood, are ladders to climb, are dismantled. However, we can never understand what is happening until we see the assault as primarily spiritual and the object of its attack being the soul and its relation to God. It is to sever this relationship that is the purpose of everything else. Jesus said, "Seek ye first the kingdom of heaven and all else will be added to you." He could just as well have said, "Abandon the search for the kingdom of heaven and you will lose everything else." We would do well to bear this in mind. It is no good resisting communism if you do not do so with the full remembrance of God for what communism is chiefly all about is the replacement of God with man, but man in his fallen mode. This is how we can easily identify its Satanic origin.

The last few chapters have referenced the End Times in terms of their effect on the West because that is where my experience lies and where most readers of this book will be living. But they affect everywhere in the world even if it is true that their greatest impact seems currently to be in the West, the home of Christianity. But nowhere escapes the prevailing winds of materialism and the dismantling of traditional hierarchies. How could that be, given that this is a phenomenon of time itself? One should also add in the light of recent political kickbacks against some aspects of decline (written in January 2025), that these are inevitable but do not alter the general direction the world is taking. Those who think political change can stop the rot have misunderstood the gravity of the situation. It's like switching from east to west when you need to go north. That these reactions succeed might even be considered as part of a tactic to divert energy away from where it should really be going into channels in which it will simply dissipate. We need to remember the devil can play for both sides in the outer world, and should not mistake the afterglow of the setting sun for a new dawn.

Not Going Along with the Aquarian Flow

Ever since I first became interested in mysticism and the esoteric, I have noticed that spiritual seekers who like to think of themselves as in some way advanced and progressive will often define themselves as Aquarians, displaying characteristics associated with that astrological sign. Hence, they will be humanitarian, egalitarian, tradition rejecting, happy to involve technology in their spiritual lives, tolerant of sexual abnormalities and so on. This is in line with the idea, now firmly established in even conventional thought, that we are leaving the Age of Pisces, associated with Christianity, and entering the Age of Aquarius in which the spiritual path takes a more universal and inclusive form. Those who can be identified as Piscean in their thinking and spiritual approach will be regarded as outmoded and behind the times. Aquarians are the vanguard of the brave new world.

I do not doubt that there are such things as astrological ages which depend on the movement of the vernal point, where the sun rises in spring in the Northern hemisphere, from one constellation to another. Since each astrological constellation spans roughly 30 degrees of the sky and the whole cycle takes around 25,800 years, the so-called Platonic or Great Year which is the name for the period during which all the fixed stars return to the position in the sky they occupied at the beginning of the cycle, the sun will rise in each sign for roughly 2000 years during which time human consciousness and civilisations will be marked by the characteristics of that particular sign. In traditional astrology each sign occupies an exact one twelfth of the whole with Aries always the first sign in spring. However, because of the slight change in direction of the Earth's polar axis over time caused by gravitational pull on the equatorial bulge or, an interesting newer theory, axial rotation of the solar system, there is the phenomenon known as the precession of the equinoxes which means that as time goes by the astrological signs and the physical constellations do not actually correspond anymore. But that doesn't matter from the point of view of geocentric astrology because Aries in this sense is not the constellation in the sky so much as the first 30 degrees after the vernal equinox.

But the physical constellation also exists, though no one really knows where one constellation ends and another begins because the boundaries are not clearly identified by any particular star. This is why we cannot know for sure when Pisces ends and Aquarius begins. It is noticeable, however, that Aquarian characteristics have been emerging since the 18th century, perhaps coincidental with the discovery of the planet Uranus which was soon seen as the new ruler of Aquarius, replacing Saturn. So, we may be in Aquarius now or we may still be at the end of Pisces. Whatever it is, Aquarius represents the New Age in many people's minds, and so to be Aquarian in consciousness is regarded as a good thing, a progressive thing.

However, here's a thought. Why should new necessarily be better? If you regard humanity as inevitably moving onwards into a better world then it might be, but traditional thought, whether Western or Eastern, has never seen the world in those terms. Christians have the End Times, Hindus have the Kali Yuga, and there are similar understandings in Buddhism and Native American lore. To think in an Aquarian way just means going with the flow, conforming to the zeitgeist, perhaps even limiting yourself to atmospheric conditions that prevail in the psychic world. Might the spiritual person be required to go beyond this or, at least, not allow himself to be bound by it? Is it not just like someone who slavishly obeys society's mores regardless of right or wrong, truth or higher truth? Should you not sometimes stand apart from those who simply go where the wind blows or the current takes them?

Aquarius as a sign has certain characteristics. These are not in themselves good or bad but can be expressed in good or bad ways. They would also need to be balanced by other signs to operate in a spiritually harmonious manner. Thus, Aquarius is innovative, egalitarian in outlook, sometimes radical, scientific, concerned with individuality and freedom. You could justifiably lay all the weirdities of wokeness at its door and some might take this as proof that these point to the future, but others would simply say that this is a perversion of the Aquarian spirit, the reaction to it on a spiritually ignorant level by immature minds.

Let me come to the point. For good or ill, we are entering the age of Aquarius. There is no reason though, certainly none that traditional spiritual thought would accept, to regard this as meaning we are entering a bright new age of love and spiritual insight. Actually, there is little of real spiritual insight in the typical Aquarian mentality. The love is mostly on a theoretical or ideological plane and the mentality involved (Aquarius is an air sign) largely intellectual. Also, we should recall that the planetary rulers of Aquarius are Saturn and Uranus. These are both, to put it completely unscientifically, quite dodgy planets. Saturn is traditionally a malefic planet which means its influence is not regarded as benign. Nowadays, we would qualify that by saying it works for the overall good but through tough love, creating hardship in order to foster development, but still, it is not sweetness and light. As for Uranus, he stands for independence, inspiration, originality, reform, unorthodoxy, eccentricity, and so on, which means he can be exciting but also unstable and disruptive. He is not safe or reliable. Consequently, both these ruling planets have problems associated with them.

The spiritually conscious person must stand above all the influences of the day. He is not to be swept along by astrological mood swings or fall into conventional ways of thinking, whatever the conventions are. He must be centred in the eternal not the temporal. The fact that the world is entering into the age of

Aquarius is irrelevant to him. Obviously, he will be affected by this as he is in the world, and to deliberately go against it is just reacting to it on a different level, but his consciousness should not be conditioned by it for it is a psychological phenomenon not a spiritual one.

The attitude that sees the age of Aquarius as heralding a new era of heightened spiritual consciousness stands in complete contrast to the traditional view in which there is a descent from a spiritually open Golden Age to a materially dominant Iron Age with the End Times wrapping things up at the conclusion of that age when the forces of Chaos overwhelm those of Order. Is there any way to reconcile these two approaches? It may be that there is when we overlay them with the Christian teaching that anticipates the reign of the Antichrist to be followed by the return of Christ and a new creation to which those who are faithful to the spirit of Christ may enter. But this is not an inevitable progression for all souls. One world ends and another begins, and to make the transition between the two the soul must align itself with Christ. Not simply believe but allow the spirit of Christ to be born in the heart. The Antichrist is the culminating point of the end times. It is a figure that seeks to draw to itself all that belongs by rights to God, and we can take it to mean either a real being or else the personification of the totality of the human ego that has severed itself from the soul. Those individuals who do not align themselves with God as represented by the figure of the returning Christ, whether that return be on the physical plane or, as some believe, on the etheric plane which we can conceive of as lying between the spiritual and the gross material and to which we would therefore have to be inwardly attuned, will gravitate to the Antichrist and so disqualify themselves from the New Age.

Thoughts on the Secular Corruption of Spirituality

I have sometimes been questioned about remarks in my books in which I condemn leftism as spiritually corrosive. I realise there are many spiritual people who would define themselves as on the left, perhaps even the majority, so let me try to explain what I mean, though the essence of it is in the title of this chapter.

First, it doesn't imply that the political right is the way to go. Spirituality lies above and beyond all politics and wants nothing to do with any of it in the sense of identifying with any party or the aims and objectives of any party. When you see this world in the light of a higher world then everything about it must be appraised in a totally different light.

That having been said, you have to ask how and where leftist ideology as it is today first originated, and the answer is that it arose in the 18th century with the specific rejection of God and his replacement with humanitarianism. Ideas that came together then may have been percolating since at least the early Middle Ages, and in England one might point to the Peasants' Revolt in 1381 and the Civil War in the mid-17th century as leftist-inspired movements, but the late 1700s is when the old order with its priorities of throne and altar really changed.

Now, this change may have been a necessary development at the time because it reflected the growth of awareness of the self throughout all sections of society. This mass awakening of the consciousness soul, as the greater awareness of self has been called, required a new approach to life and human beings and their relationships with one another.

However, that should have been in a spiritually aware context. What happened instead was that God was removed from the centre and Man, humanity, put there. What should have been a dietary supplement became the main source of nourishment, and the resultant ideology was more and more focused on this world, seeking to establish what can only be truly known in the spiritual world down here in the material. And it did this by ignoring the reality that this is a fallen world and we are sinners. I know people don't like this idea today but anyone who is honest must know it to be true. There is a spiritual corruption within all of us, and denying that fact changes nothing. The left tries to redeem fallen man as fallen man instead of getting him to transcend that state for a higher state of being. This transformation demands we see ourselves for what we are, and the left would say we are largely all right as what we are. We just need to change our outer institutions. That is just not true. It's like telling a sick man he is not sick and can be healed if he moves into a bigger house.

Spiritual people when they are on the left are so because they believe that is the compassionate approach. But what is real compassion? Consolidating someone in their ignorance or giving them the wherewithal to transcend that? Most answers to most questions were given by Jesus, and if you look at his life you will see that in some respects he acted as might a person on the left and in others as might someone on the right. That's because he was neither. He went beyond both for both are limited ideological approaches not founded in truth, and Jesus spoke from truth. A good example is when the crowd was going to stone the woman caught in adultery. Jesus stopped the stoning and forgave her (left) but also told her to sin no more (right). So, there is forgiveness but there is also the recognition of sin as sin, and the insistence on repentance.

If you boiled left and right down to their core principles you might get something like equality and freedom, and these are mutually exclusive despite the catchy slogan of the French Revolution. In fact, it is freedom that is the deep reality of the human soul. Equality is not a real thing. It never can be other than in unexpressed non-being when nothing is anything. You might say that spiritual leftists are well-meaning but even if we grant them this excuse the fact remains that they interpret spiritual reality in terms of this world when the very opposite is what is required. This does not do away with compassion but expands it by incorporating wisdom. I must re-emphasise that condemning leftism in this way does not mean recommending its rival but, insofar as the traditional right is grounded in the acknowledgement of God, it is more something that does not live up to its standards than something that has rejected those standards. And I do condemn leftism because it does seek to separate us from God, replacing him with a man-made idol if he is allowed at all. What is the difference in most things between a spiritual leftist and a worldly one? Hardly anything really, which means that the spiritual person is being influenced by the worldly one to see reality in terms of the priorities of this world.

None of this will convince anyone not already on board with it, but it might give some people trying to make sense of their instincts when these instincts are dismissed by mainstream good opinion some rational grounds to justify them.

I mentioned the 18th century as the origin of modern-day leftism, but I also said you could go back further as nothing comes from nothing. In addition to the events we have already cited, you could go back to the Reformation which introduced relativism and subjectivism into Western culture. Some of the effects of this were good or even necessary because they allowed for the greater expression of individual consciousness which was one of the primary missions of Western man, but there were also rather severe negative consequences, and these resulted in an increasingly secularised society with moral, social, and even religious values centred in the worldly human being rather than the reality of God. The immanent started to drive out the transcendent. From all this came liberalism which originally sought to free man from oppressive external authority but soon escalated to other forms until now it seeks to liberate us from both God and Nature. Will it eventually even liberate us from ourselves with the nightmare of transhumanism?

People might say what is the left of which you speak. Surely it is just the belief that human beings should be treated with fairness and compassion, and allowed to express themselves as they wish? Who could possibly not be sympathetic to that aspiration? This may be how the left presents itself initially but in reality it soon becomes purely oppositional, which does betray the adversarial spirit behind it. In our day it is against natural law and the natural order. It is anti-white, anti-male (and anti-female or, at least, anti-feminine), anti-marriage, anti-nature, anti-creation and anti-God, especially anti-God the Father. The compassion of the left is often just an excuse to deny our duty to our Creator and has more in common with an act of rebellion than one of proper love. Leftism is an ideology that could only arise in the end times when the material pole of being dominates the spiritual. This should be clear once we understand that equality is a principle of matter and not spirit, for while spirit in its pure or unmanifest state transcends both hierarchy and equality, when expressed in the context of the spirit/matter duality, in other words, when expressed creatively, it becomes the principle of hierarchy.

It is often said that when the Antichrist comes, he will be a humanitarian.

Satanic Feminism

This is the title of a book by a Swedish academic called Per Faxneld. It is published by the Oxford University Press so must be considered a work of serious research. However, I haven't read the book and am not going to because I am more concerned with the basic thesis behind it than a long excursion through history to make a single point. That point is revealed in the subtitle which is *Lucifer as the Liberator of Women in Nineteenth-Century Culture*, and the theme of the book is the link between feminism and Satan which goes right back to Eve. As far as I can tell without having read it, the book is not written from a Christian point of view and no moral conclusions are drawn. If anything, I would imagine this particular Lucifer is cast as the Promethean hero who awakens consciousness as he is regarded in certain schools of occultism, but it may well just be a scholarly look at an obscure subject.

The subject may be obscure in the overall context of 19th century history, but it has had a massive impact on the modern world. Feminism according to the official narrative is a natural result of Enlightenment concern with egalitarianism and reason, but what if it is also part of an attack on humanity and attempt to unmake the natural order of creation by something that we may as well call by the traditional name of Satan? For Christians this is an evil force that acts against the will of God and seeks to increase disorder, chaos and, ultimately, bring about spiritual dissolution, but for some people it is a liberating force that offers freedom from oppression. There are reasonable grounds for thinking it likes to present itself in this way and make an appeal thereby to human egotism, even if those who succumb to the temptation offered would cast the appeal as one to strength and individuality.

Is the devil the evil being he is depicted as in Christianity or is he a misunderstood champion of universal life who seeks to bring about evolutionary advancement in those who are bold enough to accept his challenges? Does he liberate us from servitude, or does he lure us to destruction? (Sidenote: You can see how this could also be applied to feminism.) The answer to a proper spiritual sensibility is clear. The Christian view is the correct one and those who fall for his blandishments do so because of their own egotism. They are greedy for power, and he offers it to them, but the old stories tell us that while he may give something in the short term, it is of worldly benefit only and he always claims something in return, which is the soul.

The devil always prefers a half-truth to a lie. It is much more persuasive, much more seductive. The truth that really is in it can blind us to the lie that is smuggled in and contaminates the whole idea like a worm in an apple. Where feminism is concerned, the time had come for certain changes in line with the changes in consciousness, but they should still have been in the overall context of the eternal nature of things. That may evolve but it does not change fundamentally. Just as feminists are wrong in their pursuit of a spurious equality (spurious because based on false premises), so dyed-in-the-wool traditionalists are mistaken in thinking that society should revert to a time when women were regarded as purely passive and completely subordinate to men — though in reality things were never that simple. What was required was a deeper understanding of both masculinity and femininity in their spiritual and archetypal aspects which one can begin to gain through meditation on the relationship between spirit and matter, or God and Nature which relationship contains both a hierarchical element and a complementary one, and which is the source of all creative expression. Modern feminism is like an attempt to make two suns from a sun and a moon or even, in its more extreme aspects, an attempt by the moon to swap places with the sun. It turns what should be a loving relationship of two complementary halves making a whole greater than the sum of its parts into a competitive rivalry which is spiritually damaging for them both.

If Satan really is the inspiration behind feminism, there are only two options. By being an attack on the human form, feminism is an attack on the human soul. It seeks to prise us apart from the reality of our being and therefore separate us from God. This would be the Christian view. Or else Satan is the great liberator who comes to free us from oppression, first women from men, and then all humanity from a capricious and tyrannical deity. That is how he would depict himself, but this freedom is an illusion because it makes us slaves to our ego and worldly desires. The feminist is betraying her spiritual self to further the ends of her earthly ego. She is reverting to Eve or even Lilith when she should be following Mary.

This is why from the spiritual point of view these end times can be seen as a dangerous time to be a woman. That might seem an odd statement since women have more power and freedom today than ever before, but that is the point. There is more power and freedom to reject God and the order of creation, and there is political and cultural support for doing so. A woman in the modern world must have a finely tuned spiritual sensibility to go against the prevailing winds. That doesn't mean reversion to traditional behaviour because there was always some real substance behind the push for female emancipation in the 19th century, but that does not justify the capitulation to forces of egotism, resentment, and pride, and these temptations are more powerful to the female psyche now especially since some contemporary trends in feminist ideology have led to the validation of female pathologies and the rebranding as positive virtues of such things as hatred of men, extreme emotionalism, aggressive argumentativeness, narcissism, and other examples of the negative side of femininity (in this world everything has a negative side). The traditional feminine virtues of kindness, humility, gentleness, intuitive wisdom, all summed up in the figure of the Blessed Virgin Mary, are derided as weak and submissive, concocted as ideals by men to keep women in check. At the same time, women are led into areas of life in which they must suppress their natural femininity and develop more masculine traits which merely separate them from their true selves and paths of spiritual fulfilment.

Feminism might be regarded as a test for women. For both sexes, but mostly for women. It is rather like giving someone a lot of money or power and seeing how they react to it. I am reminded of Jesus's saying that it is harder for the rich to get into heaven than for a camel to go through the eye of a needle. Richness is not just about money. It is also about power, and women have more of both these days and are correspondingly more at risk of spiritual loss.

This is why it is a spiritually dangerous time to be a woman. You have been given what you want or what you think you want. It seems good, but there is a catch which concerns your soul. You have exchanged spiritual benefit for worldly power. The other side of this is that those women who see through this temptation will make considerable spiritual advances. As for men, they should reject feminism but do so for the right reasons which means acknowledging that men and women both represent fundamental aspects of God's creation and, though their roles are not the same, they are equally valuable. The wise and the foolish understand this, albeit in different ways. The merely clever, of whom there are many these days, do not. Modern education has a lot to answer for.

The accusation of misogyny is often used to disarm those who simply point out the disorders of female psychology while doing the same for men is acceptable. Those who uphold the traditional Christian (or just traditional) view of the roles of the two sexes are similarly dismissed. It's yet another weaponised word (racism, sexism etc.) which is used to shut down argument and score points without being required to demonstrate truth. All radical political movements seek to capture and control language, and it is important in any fightback not to be bound by the linguistic conventions of the new ideology which only exist to force the argument into certain predetermined channels. While no one could deny that male misogyny exists, feminism can also be a form of misogyny. We know that Satan fears woman when she is oriented to God because then he has no power over her, and she can inspire man to right action. This is why he seeks to corrupt her, and through her man as well.

Divine Femininity

In the end times natural hierarchies are first levelled then overturned because of the veiling of spirit which is the masculine pole of being. This is why all modern beliefs and assumptions should be subjected to metaphysical analysis to see if they hold up from the perspective of First Principles, which, it should be noted, cannot be proved, only known. It may be that some developments do bring out aspects of reality that have been neglected but it is more probable, given the end times degradation of the environment on all levels not just the physical, that radical revolutions in thought contravene the natural order of the cosmos.

Feminism was a radical revolution, overturning thousands of years of a cultural norm that existed everywhere in the world. I don't think people today really appreciate that. We in the secular West are so used to it and take it so much for granted that we never question it as perhaps we should. A spiritually aware person, and especially a Christian, cannot fail to see that feminism arose concurrently with the rejection of God. It goes against traditional teaching of all religions, which may be a bad thing or a good thing, but should give us a reason to examine its origins more deeply than we normally do.

My contention would be that a change in consciousness that was of divine inspiration and had an evolutionary purpose was hijacked by a counter-evolutionary force. Around 250 years ago developments that had been gathering pace started to come to full expression. A new form of consciousness, one that had appeared here and there for hundreds of years in pioneers of humanity, began to spread more widely and to impact the whole of society and culture. This was when the 'I' became fully aware of itself and of its ability to think and to act. No longer part of a tribe or group, it was now a full individual as a result of which it became spiritually cut off from the rest of the universe. A famous precursor of this form of consciousness would be the figure of Hamlet, often called the first modern person, but now it had spread throughout all human beings, especially, to begin with, those in the West, and it led to the questioning of religion and the assertion of self. It had certain benefits as people began to act independently, the development of science for one, but it also increased the sense of alienation. It was an advance because moving from group consciousness to self-consciousness is a necessary step to full and active participation in divine life, but it also brought trouble in its wake as the separation from God became absolute. You cannot know yourself properly and be fully conscious of yourself if you retain the greater connection to universal life but when you lose that connection you may well be plunged into isolation and existential loneliness.

This change in consciousness lies behind most things of the modern era, good and bad. It was the cause of what became feminism because it was experienced by men and women alike who both now had to negotiate life and relationships from a new standpoint. Feminism from this perspective is an inevitable consequence of evolutionary development. As women become more aware of themselves as full individuals in a similar way to men so their inner life changes and that means their outer life must change too.

Therefore, the impulse behind feminism in its origin was not Satanic. But what if the change prompted by that impulse was captured and rerouted? There are two forces in the universe, not two equal forces because ultimately everything comes from God, but still two forces that are in opposition. There is the divine force that seeks to bring human beings to spiritual completion and there is a counter force that we call evil because it opposes good. The aim of this evil force is to separate from God, not temporarily as in the sense of being a self-centred individual but permanently. This tells us that the current stage of full individual consciousness carries risks because if that sense of self is taken too far it can lead to a much deeper separation from God and the true good. Self-centred individuality is like adolescence, a temporary phase that should act as a springboard to a deeper adult engagement with God, but unfortunately the whole process has been derailed, and we have got stuck in that phase. This has been due to the nature of end times spiritual deterioration as well as interference from demonic sources but also, it must be said, to our own weakness.

This is the sense in which feminism can be described as Satanic. A potentially positive change was hijacked, and materialistic elements were promoted while the spiritual purpose was suppressed. The weaknesses of the worldly ego were exploited while the redirecting of greater self-awareness to spiritual awakening, proper spiritual awakening I should stress because there are many forms which are to do with the ego self-medicating, failed to take place. Sunshine and rain cause both nourishing fruits and poisonous weeds to grow, depending on the receiving soil and the seeds. A downpouring of psychic energy can be reacted to by the soul or the ego, depending on how the subject is attuned. It can also be mis-channelled by the counter-evolutionary forces which can be collectively identified under the traditional name of Satan, and this was what occurred.

What should have happened was the development of a deeper understanding of both masculinity and femininity in their inner creative aspects. If men and women had responded to this phase of consciousness on a spiritual level, they could have opened themselves up to the more archetypal qualities of Man and Woman. This would have built on tradition (the law and the prophets) instead of doing away with it. Feminism, as we know it, is a perversion of a good. Its origins do lie in a certain truth, but that truth has been corrupted. For Man and Woman are the two fundamental pillars of creation, equal in spiritual worth, different in spiritual function. The Satanic element of feminism is the confusion of worth and function.

Feminism is a metaphysical matter not a political, social, or humanistic one, and the failure to understand that is the cause of confusion. It is why people whose worldview is based on modernity and secularism have made the misguided choices they have. To such people a position such as the one I have outlined here will seem bad because it conflicts with their idea of good, but if you lack metaphysical understanding, you cannot know what the real good is. There truly are feminine mysteries but these have been discarded and rejected by feminism as they can only be known through humility and submission to God as demonstrated by Mary in her response to the angel Gabriel at the annunciation. The old goddesses dear to the modern feminist may represent aspects of the female psyche but they do not represent its higher spiritual reality nor that towards which it should be evolving. Feminine spirituality is certainly tied to the moon but that means it is best realised through submission to the higher forces outside her being as opposed to the solar path of the male which primarily involves conquering the lower forces within.

Only when we do approach the question of man and woman from the metaphysical perspective can we understand the significance of the two sexes. Woman to Man is the cosmic mystery that lies within creation, which includes the mysteries of birth and death. Man to Woman is life itself and God. For the Cosmic Masculine in the male/female polarity represents the transcendent One when it manifests outwardly, while the Feminine arises when life moves into duality and expression as the immanence of the divine and the ground of Nature. And this is the reason, arguing from first principles, why feminism is an aberration which could only arise in a time of spiritual ignorance.

The Cassandra Syndrome

It seems a common experience that when those who have some understanding of the nature of the present times speak about the parlous state of the world, the country, the culture, or just the human soul, they are met with incomprehension or denial. Most people simply cannot accept that the Western world in the 21st century stands on the edge of a precipice. They may worry about the economy or the climate, but they do not see that the rot is far deeper.

Cassandra, as I am sure you know, was a Trojan princess who was cursed by the god Apollo after he had given her the gift of prophecy in exchange for sexual favours which she then withheld. Her fate thereafter was that everything she prophesied would be true, but no one would believe her. This has echoes of Mark 6:4 when Jesus said that a prophet is not without honour except in his own country and among his own kin. You don't have to be a prophet now to see that the spiritual state of the world is dire. Anyone who has the slightest awareness of reality ought to be able to see it. The remarkable thing is most people don't, and one is tempted to say they won't either. They refuse to do so because they are too firmly ensconced in their own comfortable pseudo-reality. They will go along with the clearly biased and fictitious mainstream narrative as we saw in the events of 2020 and have seen again since on various occasions, and get quite angry if holes in these narratives are presented to them. They will talk about science when it appears to back them up but reject it when it does not.

Why is this? One reason is that most people are still cushioned by the comfort of relative wealth. As long as the trains run on time, so to speak, they will believe everything is fine not realising that when an electric fan is turned off the blades continue to rotate for a while but increasingly slowly until they stop. The time to be concerned is when the current is cut not when the blades stop, by which time it will be too late.

Then we live in a culture which no longer has objective truth as a priority. It is replaced by a relativistic attitude in which there is no higher or lower, but everybody must be accepted on their own terms because we're all equal. That way we all get along, supposedly. In such a nursery world truth can seem hard and ugly, threatening even, and so you ignore it, but truth is what is, and what is cannot be denied. If you do deny it, you will only bring greater suffering on yourself in the long term. The Trojans ignored Cassandra when she warned them about the Horse left behind by the Greeks. They brought it inside their gates and its foreign occupants destroyed them, a parallel which should give us pause for thought today.

And then most people now have zero awareness of the spiritual reality of things. Religion has been destroyed in many places in the Western world, and the tried and tested traditional wisdom of the past has been sidelined for fashionable dogma. The takeover of the country's institutions, political, legal, educational, the media, by the forces of atheism and materialism is now complete. Some commentators speculate that these institutions have been the victims of deliberate sabotage because of Communist infiltration, and the process has been so insidious and so comprehensive that this seems a reasonable explanation. However, we still need to recognise that the agents carrying out the scheme in this world are the servants not the masters which doesn't make them any better, but we should know the ultimate source of the evil and that is supernatural.

How have they got away with this? One answer is suggested by Yeats in his prophetic poem "The Second Coming" when he sums up the situation in a couple of lines that have become well-known. *"The best lack all conviction, while the worst are full of passionate intensity."* I'm not sure that the best lack conviction but the majority surely does and so leaves itself open to the machinations of the passionate worst. Evil hates good which gives it its passionate intensity but most people's connection to the good is too feeble to make them fight for it, and this is doubly so when they have been indoctrinated to believe that fighting is morally wrong because to fight is to hate. And so, we are left with the strange situation in which actual hatred disguises itself as love and condemns supposed hatred, in reality love of the good, in order to delegitimise any opposition to itself.

But we must fight for truth when it is under assault, and we mustn't be afraid to appear unloving when we do so long as we fight from love of the good. Listen to what Jesus has to say in John 8:44 about the Pharisees of whom there are still a great many around today.

> *You are from your father the devil, and you choose to do your father's desires. He was a murderer from the beginning and does not stand in the truth, because there is no truth in him. When he lies, he speaks according to his own nature, for he is a liar and the father of lies.*

Isn't this hate speech, to use an emotive modern term? Maybe, but it comes from the Apostle of Love which should make us pause for thought. The fact is there is evil. It has a spiritual source, and it must be recognised for what it is and fought with all our strength.

The Trojans refused to listen to Cassandra because she disturbed them. They would rather close their minds to truth than accept reality because reality challenged their comfortable illusions. Most prophets bring bad news – that, after all, is their function, to call an erring community back to God. But

Cassandra was right, and if the Trojans had listened to her, they might have avoided their destruction.

Cassandra lived during a kind of end times. It was the destruction of Troy and roughly contemporaneous with what is known as the Late Bronze Age Collapse when numerous societies in the Eastern Mediterranean and Near East experienced catastrophic decline. Not only Troy but many other city states had violent endings, including Mycenae in Greece. Even ancient Egypt was shaken, never fully to recover its former power. Famine and drought caused by a combination of earthquakes and climate change, themselves possibly the result of some kind of cometary impact, was probably the primary reason for societal breakdown, and it could have been this that instigated the violence as groups of people migrated from their homelands in search of food.

Dated to around 1200 BC, this collapse can be seen as the end of an age not just in terms of the metal used but culturally as well. When a new world arose, iron replaced bronze as the metal of choice, but perhaps more relevant to our theme is that humanity seemed to have lost its contact with the supernatural. The Bronze Age was the age of myths, gods, and heroes but these now had all faded into the past, and with the rise of the classical age in Greece the seeds of modernity were sown.

In my earlier book *Earth is a School*, following the author Robert Bolton, I gave speculative dates for the Kali Yuga as running from 3102 BC to 2082 AD. All this period would correspond to the Iron Age using that phrase in the sense given it by Hesiod rather than the more conventional metallurgical sense. Hesiod spoke of humanity as living through a cycle of four main ages that ran from Gold to Silver to Bronze to Iron. The Gold Age is an earthly paradise of ease and bounty, but we then descend to ever more material states of being with a corresponding deterioration in spiritual awareness and moral sensibility until in the Iron Age, in which Hesiod thought himself to be living, life is hard and wrongdoing abounds. Hesiod interpolates a Heroic Age between Bronze and Iron which seems a brief recapitulation of earlier times and an interruption of general decline, but it only arrests the downward trend temporarily.

We can equate the Kali Yuga and the Iron Age, and that means we have been in this period of spiritual barrenness for five thousand years. However, there are two points to note. Firstly, we are nearing the end of it and entering a time at which the pace of decline accelerates as the momentum built up from several millennia of materialisation gathers pace. Secondly, Bolton proposes the interesting theory that within the major cycle there are minor cycles which repeat the general pattern of the major. He breaks them down in the proportions 4,3,2,1 which correspond to the relative lengths of the major components of the cycle so the Golden Age of the Kali Yuga would last, according to his dates, for 2076 years from 3103 BC to 1026 BC, which is close enough to the Late Bronze Age Collapse to be interesting. We then entered the Silver Age of the Kali Yuga and that would correspond to the historical Iron Age.

The end times is the tail of the Hesodian Iron Age which, if we accept Bolton's dates, would be around now. There have been previous minor end times, such as the late Bronze Age Collapse, when minor cycles within the main cycle came to a finish, but now is the end of the main cycle. The Silver section of the Iron Age ended in 528 AD, which is near enough to the time that the western Roman empire fell and the European Dark Ages began, and the Bronze of Iron period concluded in 1564 AD, which will do very well for the end of the Middle Ages and separation from the supernatural element of Christianity, which was one of the main consequences of the Reformation. But now a minor cycle, a major cycle, and the whole cycle are all coming to an end, which is why the entire world will be affected. In fact, the very last phase is due to start in 2030 so we can look forward to interesting times soon. The process has been underway for a while, but if you want a date for when the end times really get going then that is as good as any.

Part Two

Spiritual Tradition

Introduction on What Tradition Is

There is Tradition and there are traditions. The various traditions are attempts to express Tradition in a particular place and at a particular time. They are better or worse approximations of the source to which they seek to conform themselves, but they have this in common. They recognise a transcendent divine reality and the need for a culture to try to attune itself to that reality, and pattern itself on the order of creation. Most societies did this in their various ways but the modern world, almost uniquely, neither follows the order of creation nor accepts the transcendent reality. The result is Tradition is lost but there is worse to come, for following its loss there is deliberate subversion of Tradition by forces inimical to it. These forces have always existed but have been held back by the power of Tradition. Without that safeguard they are let loose. One of the ways by which we can identify the end times is the degree to which this undermining of Tradition has taken effect. It is right that traditions get reviewed in the light of the present because they can ossify so that the letter becomes more important than the spirit, but to reject the spirit as well as the letter, the form in which the spirit is presented, is a sign of both intellectual and moral decay.

When a society closes itself to Tradition, or transcendence which amounts to the same thing, what happens is twofold. First, that society becomes trapped in the material world, but then psychic forces from below the level of everyday consciousness start to erupt into the sphere of regular perceived reality. Materialism shuts off access to the true spiritual via its denial of Tradition so a false spiritual appears as a substitute since man cannot live by bread alone. However, this seeps in from below as the path to higher regions is blocked. Many signs of this are evident in the fields of art and spirituality and elsewhere.

The next few chapters concern the loss of Tradition in the end times and some of the consequences of that. We should note that even where some connection to Tradition remains in the form of a tradition it often remains in a debased state so that its value is much reduced and can even be counterproductive. This is why the true seeker in these end times must strike a solitary path, absorbing what he can from the traditions that exist but realising that these are increasingly lanterns that have lost their light. Following the general pattern of the end times in which quantity presides over quality we find we have greater access to all manner of traditions now from widely ranging times and places, but their redemptive powers have waned considerably. It's as though the wider they are spread, the shallower they become, but it is also because the living energy that informed them has dissipated over time.

Today, Western Man finds himself in a spiritual void. He has rejected his Christian inheritance and filled the gap with the ideological fantasies of materialism plus a lot of technological toys without which the emptiness of his materialism would soon reveal itself. The marvels of technology can stave off the awareness of emptiness for a while but not forever, and the loss of Tradition is increasingly felt because this is all that can offer real substance to the soul. The question is, do we deal with that by returning to the source and the reality which Tradition sought to express, or do we resort to one of the many palliatives and fake substitutes on offer today?

René Guénon was the founder of the school of thought known as Traditionalists, and among the first to point to the spiritual degradation of modernity. He wrote eloquently on the end times or the Reign of Quantity as he fittingly described it in the title of his best-known work. He converted to Islam because it uncompromisingly resisted modernity and seemed to maintain, or so he thought, a relatively uncontaminated contact with Tradition. But modernity arose from a positive value which was the growth of self-consciousness, and, although it became spiritually rotten, the core of truth at its heart cannot be denied. Guénon did not appear to understand that Islam is an evolutionarily static remnant from the past, and to turn to it in reaction to the spiritual problems of the present is no solution at all. It may be a tradition that has kept a better contact than most with its origin, but as a religion it was always limited and never suitable for the West, founded in freedom and individuality, anyway, which is why it had to be repulsed in the Middle Ages and should be resisted now. Surviving the end times is not about aligning oneself with an outmoded traditional form but going inwards and contacting the living spirit of Tradition for yourself.

The Temptation of the Esoteric

Ancient mysteries, hidden secrets, the wisdom of the ancients. Whose imagination isn't stirred by the idea of arcane knowledge preserved by initiates of the distant past? The magic of Egypt, the mysticism of India, the occultism of Tibet can all be powerful drugs to the questing mind seeking to penetrate the veil between this world and the next. It's intoxicating stuff and there undoubtedly is a reality behind it all. It's not just dreams and fantasy. But is it what spirituality is about, especially for us here and now in the modern West?

It's just a coincidence but esoteric and exotic do sound rather similar, and it's not just the words that are alike. They both conjure up the sense of something fascinating and strange that can reveal unsuspected new areas of experience. They can take you beyond the mundane and everyday, and give you a pleasant feeling of superiority over ordinary people if you explore or, better yet, possess them.

Wise teachers have always warned of the difference between magic and religion. The esoteric, if outside the context of religion, has much in common with magic in that it is to do with knowledge and power. It certainly appeals to those who hunger for these things and who may be motivated by that hunger rather than a pure aspiration to truth. I am reminded of the saying that spiritual truth is simple, but it is easy to get lost in philosophical speculations which lead nowhere. And not just philosophical speculations. Anything that is not inspired by the love of God is a spiritual sidetrack, and the esotericist is often a long way from simple faith and worship, using the word worship in its proper sense which is loving God.

Everything changed with the advent of Christ. This becomes more apparent as the world sinks into spiritual darkness and Christ is neglected not just by the general populace but by the churches that preach in his name. Before the time of Christ there were many forms of spirituality, and they could open doors into the unknown for the qualified initiate, but they did not lead to Heaven. This is why Dante confines even the wise and virtuous Virgil to Limbo. Those who go back to the past without fully accepting Christ are not revivifying ancient teachings that will give them access to the Mysteries. The spirit has departed from them. It was once present but is no longer, and though you may be able to recreate a simulacrum of the once living and vital truth embodied by these spiritual forms, you will not find the living truth itself. That is now in Christ.

I don't know much about Freemasonry, but I imagine this is why it is condemned by the Catholic Church. No doubt there is a kernel of esoteric wisdom behind its ceremonies and rituals, possibly passed down from ancient Egypt though it will have travelled a long way since then and been subject to the Chinese whispers effect. Nevertheless, there will be something there. However, if Christ is not there, and as far as I can tell he isn't, that renders the whole enterprise suspect. Hidden truth without Christ is not truth. Write that down and memorise it. Moreover, in the case of Freemasonry, it has always been too concerned with building a New World Order, and this ambition, pursued today by the globalism of the oligarchs, has long been seen as part of the attempt to provide a platform for the Antichrist when he comes. Even if you find that far-fetched you cannot ignore the strong whiff of a Tower of Babel given off by Freemasonry.

I am not condemning the esoteric. We are called to knowledge, and we should seek it out. Knowledge is not just our spiritual right but to pursue it is our duty too. Greater knowledge will enable us to interact with God and the universe on a deeper level. I have explored esoteric teachings for over 40 years as is easy nowadays when so much has been published and made available to anyone who can read, one of the actual advantages of living in the end times. But I do say that if we do this, we should do it under the banner of Christ or we risk falling into illusion and worse. In the end times much that was hidden stands revealed but the traditional forms of protection have been removed or lost. Christ remains the universal protection for those who would enter the unseen world.

Having said all that, let us look at this question from another angle. For while the study of the esoteric cannot substitute for a proper religious attitude it can be a great aid to that, especially now when all religions have lost contact with their originating animating inspiration and become dusty relics of the past. Esoteric understanding may be neither sufficient nor necessary for salvation, but it can be very helpful and, though the intellectual mind is not the key to unlocking the door of spiritual truth, it can guide the key to the lock.

Faith and knowledge are often separated and regarded as almost in opposition to one another, but they are more like man and woman with each one complementing and deepening the other. Without faith, knowledge is dry and spiritually sterile. Without knowledge, faith can be impotent and immature and rooted in ignorance. Ignorance is never good. It will likely lead to error and then becomes faith in what is false. What use is that?

Esoteric teachings are simply a guide to the higher aspects of the human being: where we have come from, where we should be going, and how we get to there from here. Then they describe the spiritual structure of the universe. They are, properly considered, the knowledge aspect of religion and so are a form of spiritual science. Like material science they can be abused but in themselves they are good because they are founded on truth, though I would add the proviso that any teaching calling itself esoteric needs to be subjected to the rigour of intuition, common sense, and cast in the light of the reality of Christ. If it conflicts with the latter, it should be treated with circumspection.

There may have been a time when knowledge of the higher worlds was relatively unimportant for the work we need to do in this world to grow and develop spiritually but now human beings have evolved their minds, and the mind needs to be catered for. It must have food. If it does not have real knowledge, it will have false knowledge and it will act according to that in ways that would not have been possible before as it has more agency. Consequently, it will do more harm. So, you could say that esoteric understanding has become more important than it was, and for everyone not just the advanced soul. A developing mind must have something to know.

Moreover, there is a God-given impulse in the mind pushing it towards growth. We need to understand. We are in fact obliged to understand, and esoteric teachings provide some form of understanding. They are not perfect because we are still very limited beings, but we are growing towards the light and esoteric teachings can be a kind of fertiliser that help us to grow so long as they are balanced by growth in the spiritual and moral sense.

It is no accident that much of what was esoteric has been revealed in the end times. This is a time when everything comes to the surface, but the inevitable danger is the trivialisation and vulgarisation that takes place with the democratisation of spiritual knowledge. Still, we have been given access to something that will serve us well if we respond to it correctly. Esotericism can provide clarity to the mind, but it needs to be balanced by purity of the heart. Clarity and purity. These are the requirements for the modern disciple if he would survive the end times without spiritual hurt.

Buddhist Atheism

In one sense original Buddhism is the purest of all religions for it strips away everything except naked spirit. All the extraneous elements of the spiritual search were seen by the Buddha as obscuring the central reality of existence, the underlying causeless cause of the countless worlds of phenomenal manifestation. He realised that the world was in a condition of constant decay and sought the pristine state of incorruptible being that could never be violated by change or loss or evil. By sheer force of spiritual will coupled with absolute sincerity of motive and integrity of mind, he broke through the many veils overlaying consciousness and entered the innermost sanctuary of life where darkness and light had not yet been divided. He attained the perfect knowledge that comes from merging individual being with the universal I AM. His supreme achievement opened a door between the created and uncreated worlds allowing others who were spiritually developed enough to follow in his footsteps, but he was the first to scale this spiritual Everest.

Those who have been to a South Indian temple will know that the outer sections contain halls and courts with carved pillars and statues in which all the important elements of life are represented, both material and spiritual. The decoration is elaborate showing the almost profligate abundance of life, every aspect of which is celebrated to the consternation of some early European visitors. But in the innermost part of the temple there is a sparsely decorated or even bare cell-like chamber without window or light. This is called the womb chamber and is where the image of the presiding deity stands. There, the *Murti* or earthly embodiment of the god or goddess (Christians would call it an idol forgetting that there are representations of Jesus, Mary, and the saints in Christianity too) is tended by the priests and worshipped by the faithful. However, what many of the ordinary worshippers might not be aware of is that this dark and empty space, void of decoration and without form of any kind, that houses the deity and from which the deity might be said to take its rise represents *Purusa* which in the Hindu tradition is pure spirit, the essential reality of all things. The Buddha focused his attention entirely on this, going beyond all the paraphernalia of the temple, all the ritual, even beyond the deity itself, to the very ground that gives birth to creation.

The Buddha was the apostle of enlightenment which is the perfection of wisdom. He introduced this wisdom into the oversoul of humanity, its collective super-consciousness, enabling those who followed him and who were responsive enough to build it into their own minds. When Christ came, he introduced humanity to the spiritual quality of love, allowing those who attuned themselves to his divine nature to partake of this love themselves. Christ went further than the Buddha because he sanctified matter, including the human self, and original Buddhism did not do this. It left it behind as corrupt. This is not to denigrate Buddhism since the Buddha was the one who struck the first blow against the corruption inherent in the material world since the Fall, opening up a path out of matter into spirit. Christ then came to heal the sickness in matter so it could be reunited with spirit, but perhaps he might not have been able to do this without the Buddha's initial opening of the way to spirit. Might one even see these two great beings working in tandem for the upliftment of humanity? This is not to dispute Christ's uniqueness as the Son of God nor his pre-eminence, but to do his work he needed the spiritual ground to be prepared, and this it was not only by the teachings of the Hebrew prophets from the Old Testament but also by all the spiritual endeavours of humanity up to that point, the greatest of which was that of the Buddha.

Buddhism has made a big impact in the West since its introduction but, notwithstanding all the above, there are problems with Buddhism especially when imported into the West. In my earliest days of spiritual exploration, I went to a Buddhist meditation centre in London and was told there was no such thing as the self. Buddhists will say that the Buddha neither affirmed nor denied the reality of the individual self and that's true enough as far as it goes, but the effective reality of the Buddhist path is that the self is denied. This is a major problem for the Western psyche, and not because of the shortcomings of that psyche but because of its virtues and what it is intended to achieve.

I left this centre convinced that their philosophy was mistaken. I understood the idea that there is a supernal state of consciousness beyond the limitations of the ego or the phenomenal self, but this does not mean that the individual human being, the soul, has no reality. According to the Christian view which goes more deeply into the question (it really does), the individual soul is the whole point of creation, and note that if Buddhism were correct there would be no point to creation, no meaning in it. It is through the soul's experience in this world in which subject and object have been split apart that it can reach a state, Heaven, that is beyond the condition of pure spiritual oneness in that it is a state of loving relationship both with God, the supreme I AM of the universe, and with other souls. This would not be possible or even desirable in pure Buddhism, but is a far richer, more meaningful and more creative state than resting in the changeless perfection of Nirvana.

Without God the tendency is to make gods of ourselves. The two approaches to that are those of Satan and the Buddha though in no way am I comparing the two. Satan fell into evil and the attempt to deify the separate self, while the Buddha went beyond good and evil into the denial of self. But God created the world and saw that it was good. It is to bring to reality the qualities of goodness, beauty, and love that God created the world and human beings. We can go back to the primeval uncreated state, which is the path of Buddhism, or we can go forward through creation into Heaven which brings together in a holy matrimony the perfection of the One, Spirit, and the beauty of the Many, matter.

Despite all its virtues, there is a sense in which Buddhism is materialistic. I realise that describing it thus might seem strange when I also say it denies the material world, a.k.a. creation, and takes its stand in pure spirit, but let us see why this might be the case. To begin with, the Buddhist definition of reality projects qualities of material things, impermanence, ultimate emptiness, fundamental meaninglessness, onto spirit so spirit becomes an example of rarified matter rather than matter being condensed spirit which is closer to the truth. You might think there is no fundamental difference between these two concepts but there surely is if you see spirit in terms of matter instead of vice versa. This is why Western atheists can be drawn to Buddhism. They don't have to change very much because their materialism is expanded from the base instead of being blasted by a ray of light from above.

This brings us to the second point, which is the rejection of God, and God is rejected in Buddhism because he is not fully acknowledged. Could it be that the rejection of God means Buddhism misconceives both spirit and matter, seeing them as philosophical abstractions rather than concrete realities? And this leads it to perceive life as made up of energies rather than beings. Buddhism might be said to transfer the impersonal nature of matter onto spirit whereas the Christian vision sees spirit as fully, gloriously, magnificently personal, and it brings that down into creation as revealed in the figure of Christ himself.

None of this is written in an anti-Buddhist spirit, but there are real spiritual difficulties with Buddhism because of its lack of a God as well as other elements compatible with materialistic atheism, and these mean it can be captured by the end times inversion of spirit and matter. The fact that for the Buddhist nothing has an abiding centre, everything is in flux, and human identity is ultimately non-existent can make it seem a spiritualised materialism with the Buddhist version of spirit very like matter with everything stripped out of it rather than something positive. Obviously, that's not what the Buddha meant but there is a built-in tendency for the Buddhist approach to become like that, and this is down to the absence of God. In the end times, many of those who are drawn to spirituality want it on their own terms which are the terms of materialistic atheism, and they take that mindset with them. They seek spirituality for healing or enlightenment, that's to say for the benefit of the self, but in these times more than ever the motivating force must be love of God. That is the meaning behind the ancient Indian tradition that in the Kali Yuga all the seeker need do to be saved is recite the name of God. It seems childishly simple but what this is saying is that in a time of universal spiritual dissolution only love for God can rescue the soul.

Buddhism is a profound philosophy but in the end times it should be regarded more as a waystation than a destination, and especially so for the Westerner. That is because of its extreme apophatic nature. God may not be an old man with a long white beard, but he is more an old man with a long white beard than nothing at all. The emptiness of Nirvana falls short of the fullness of Christ, and one of the benefits of the end times is that its spiritually corrupted nature brings to the surface all that is not Christ so the division between Christ and not-Christ becomes more clearly defined. Buddhism doesn't fall short by much but ultimately it does fall short. Its virtue, that it goes beyond the personal, becomes its Achilles heel for Christ also went beyond the personal but in doing so he took it with him, redeemed and transformed, not left behind to wither and die in the worldly dust.

Heaven, Hell, and What's In Between

We have alluded in these pages to the idea of evolving consciousness. It is for this purpose that human souls, which are spiritual beings, are subjected to the seeming indignity of incarnation in a material world, a world of evil and suffering or one where these things are potentially possible and in these latter days extremely likely. The concept of the various ages which we get from the Greek poet Hesiod and elsewhere also plays into the idea of consciousness evolving. You might think it does just the opposite, but that is because it describes a process in which both the environment and consciousness become increasingly degraded or materialised which amounts to the same thing. Thus, there is a spiritual descent but at the same time and as a result there is a development of reason and ego, as the separation between the spiritual and the material becomes more pronounced, which gives the individual ego the chance to grow, and reason, which is how a human being cut off from natural oneness seeks understanding, the space to develop. Individual consciousness must be transcended as a centre of focus, but before that can be done properly, it must be known totally. It must be gone through to be gone beyond for it provides the vehicle in which a developed spiritual understanding can be built. For the higher spiritual faculties such as intellectual insight can only be accessed and known consciously by those functioning above the threshold of egoic awareness. Below that all is automatic and instinctive.

Let us remind ourselves of Hesiod's scheme of things. In his poem *Works and Days*, he describes several Ages of Man going from Gold to Silver to Bronze to Iron with each age signifying a descent in human happiness, goodness, and nobility. The men of the Golden Age are wise, pious, and benevolent, while the Silver Age population start off reasonably well but are eventually destroyed for their impiety before the gods. There follow the men of the Bronze Age, but they descend into violence and their end comes in a great flood. Finally, we arrive at the Iron Age when life is just hard grind. There is no honour among men who lie and feel no shame. It's a sad and sorry time for everyone.

The Roman poet Ovid tells a similar story. He says that the Golden Age was a time of justice, peace, and innocence. Humanity was naturally good, but it knew little of the arts and sciences. These came about in the Silver Age as a gift from Jupiter who took over from Chronos or Saturn as the principal deity. Once again, the Bronze Age is a time of war though Ovid says men still respected the gods. However, religious feeling is quite lost in the Iron Age which becomes the most materialistic of times as men dig mines deep into the earth in their search for prosperity, that being all they care about. Truth and decency are distinguished only by their absence.

This is the Classical version of end times theory, and it seems that here there is no point to it. It's just an inevitable degradation of the world and mankind. And there certainly is that aspect to it, but just as God can use evil to bring about greater good, so the materialisation of consciousness can help advance certain aspects of the divine plan. The plan is to make gods, and gods must be fully self-conscious. To be a god is to be creative and to be creative means to be self-conscious. Self-consciousness requires separation, for a time, at least, as it develops, but it is this separation that eventually paves the way to final completion for those willing to take the steps required and overcome the separation by overcoming self. We must build up the temple of our own soul from the inside but then vacate it so that the spirit of God may illuminate it from within. It is the increasing distance from spirit as the ages progress that gives us the space to construct our own individual identity — even if that identification must eventually be transcended.

So much for the idea of evolving consciousness and how it relates to the teaching of the various ages. But how do we square this idea with the doctrine that if we reject Christ, we suffer a spiritual consequence in the afterlife, traditionally known as damnation or hell? Let us first make clear that nobody is sent to hell. You send yourself there and you do so by closing off your mind to Heaven. In Dante's vision there are different hells equating to different sins and this is because in the afterlife the principle of like attracts like operates with an individual's perceived environment reflecting his inner consciousness. The universe is a thought. Life is Mind, and in the spiritual world what you think is what you are and where you seem to be. So, there may be hells which are not necessarily that unpleasant, at least not to those who go there, but which are nevertheless deprived of God and real goodness and beauty. Which means, of course, they would be unpleasant to the reasonable person whose consciousness has not been perverted by a misdirected will, but they may not be perceived as such by those whose consciousness corresponds to them.

This world is a world of choice. You choose whether to believe in God, and you also choose what sort of God you believe in. You choose or don't choose to acknowledge Christ, and you also choose what sort of Christ to believe in because many people believe in their own version of Christ, a Christ who is a projection of their own thoughts and desires. There is the real Christ to whom you respond in the heart through the spiritual imagination, aided by scripture and even art (that is art's highest function), and there is a human created image of Christ who may be modelled on aspects of the real Christ but has some extra elements superimposed as well as important elements missing. It is a mental version of a spiritual reality and, depending on its approximation to the real Christ, does only limited good. It may even do harm if the image departs too much from the reality, and reflects more of social or political or personal concerns than spiritual truth.

Hell is separation from God. It is the separation of self-consciousness taken to extremes. There are many degrees of separation and different souls will have separated themselves to different degrees. Some will be a long way off while others may retain some kind of connection to some aspect of God, maybe a love for beauty or concern with right behaviour. For them there is a way back if they will take it, but it will mean opening closed areas of the heart and mind, and that may be more difficult in the post-mortem state as we may then have solidified choice meaning the occasion for choosing is past as the specific conditions which form the test under which you make a choice no longer prevail.

It may be that souls who refuse to accept Christ's offer of Heaven are held back on lower levels of being while others progress onwards and upwards. They don't have hell in the traditional sense, but nor do they have Heaven. It may also be that there are many such souls alive now because this is a time of reckoning when final chances are offered to souls who have turned down previous offers. Between Heaven and Hell there are many other spiritual states which are, returning to Dante, forms of Limbo which was Virgil's region in the afterlife. Virgil represented the best of humanity without God. He was virtuous and wise but he did not know Christ so he could not enter Heaven. (As an aside, I believe that all those born before Christ are given the opportunity to know Christ either through being reborn in this world or else in some other way so I would expect that a soul of the quality of Virgil is in Heaven now as are all other worthy pagans.) Thus, nonbelievers do not necessarily go to Hell, but they are barred from Heaven by their own lack of acceptance of it.

Evolving consciousness is one thing but accepting God is another. In reality, both are necessary to make a god, but you can have one without the other. The devil has what we might reasonably call a highly evolved consciousness. There are also simple souls who believe in God but are not able to express very much of him. Evolution means we can understand more of God, and we can become more like him in terms of love, creativity, and intelligence. This is the destiny we are called to. We must grow but we can only grow as we should when we grow according to the pattern of God. To grow according to that pattern is heaven. Not to do so, however evolved you are, is hell.

Astrology, A Signpost to Creation

Anyone who makes even a half-serious study of astrology will find that the horoscope provides an accurate description of its subject. It's a system of symbols and must be interpreted in context for the fullest understanding, but creative analysis of the chart of the sky at a person's birth will always give insight into the nature and character of that person. No doubt the destiny too, but I haven't investigated that side of things in any detail. On the other hand, I have looked at many horoscopes from the psychological perspective and every one of them has given an accurate description of the person. In one case, I even went back to someone to check if he had given me the right date because chart and personality didn't tally though they did for the year before. It turned out that this person had indeed been born the year before he had said. When my children were born, I made a special case of noting the exact time so I could do the most accurate horoscope possible. This is because it is not just the date and place that matters but the time which is especially significant from the point of view of points on the horizon and zenith, Ascendant and Midheaven in astrological speak, the former indicating the way you present yourself to the world and the latter showing your direction in life. I studied the horoscopes before I knew the personalities of the children and they have proved extremely accurate. I understand things about myself much better from knowing my birth chart. I believe it would benefit everyone to study their horoscope. They would have a good insight into their character strengths and weaknesses.

In Western astrology every sign of the zodiac, signs being the constellations on the ecliptic which serve as the backdrop against which the sun, moon, and planets move over a year, is said to be ruled by a particular planet. This is because sign and planet share similar qualities. Thus, Aries was traditionally ruled by Mars, Taurus by Venus, Gemini by Mercury, Cancer by the Moon, Leo by the Sun, Virgo by Mercury, Libra by Venus, Scorpio by Mars, Sagittarius by Jupiter, Capricorn by Saturn, Aquarius by Saturn, and Pisces by Jupiter. If you know anything about astrology you will see that some of these make sense and others not so much. You have to perform some mental acrobatics to make them fit. The reason is that there are 12 signs but only 5 planets plus the sun and the moon which are counted as planets for these purposes, a planet in astrology really being something that qualifies and represents a certain energy or, in human psychological terms, aspect of the psyche. When Uranus, Neptune, and Pluto were discovered they were assigned certain qualities which, it was found, fitted much better with the signs Aquarius, Pisces, and Scorpio, and this isn't just arbitrary. Astrological practice shows it works. Incidentally, the discovery of these planets coincided with certain changes and developments in human consciousness so here we can see how astrology is a living system with room for growth.

This leaves two planets with a double rulership which implies that there remain two planets waiting to be discovered, perhaps again coinciding with changes in consciousness. These could either be very far out on the edge of the solar system or very close to the sun. They could even be planets which are not fully materialised. It seems obvious that Gemini and Mercury go together, but Venus has affinities with both Taurus and Libra so that is harder to decide. On the other hand, Virgo seems unlikely to be ruled by Mercury. The two have little in common so I suspect this is one of the signs that awaits its true ruler. That may be the planet known by esoteric astrologers as Vulcan, a so-called veiled or hidden planet close to the Sun. I am undecided about the 12th sign and its true ruler, though I expect those more learned in astrology than me have their ideas.

All this indicates that astrology is still a work in progress. New ways to analyse the chart are always being developed and tested but there are also new astronomical factors astrologers consider such as the minor planet Chiron. This is not an anything goes approach because everything must make sense and work. Nothing is arbitrary, but we are dealing with a wisdom encoded into the structure of the universe, and it would be foolish to think we have uncovered all its details.

Many Christians reject astrology as a fundamentally irreligious practice. This is a mistake though perhaps understandable given the human tendency to lapse into superstition and fatalism, and yet the Magi clearly studied the stars and their knowledge led them to the Saviour. Astrology is not a religious practice nor any kind of substitute for proper religion, but it is an excellent tool for looking at creation and understanding the psyche, and, if regarded in the light of the Creator and his purpose for mankind, has many positive contributions to make to human development. Astrology is a signpost to the *fact* of creation, that there is intelligence and purpose behind it, and method and order throughout the universe.

What relation does astrology have to the end times? You might think, given its predictive nature, that astrology could point to patterns indicating the end times in the heavens, but that does not appear to be the case, not in any clear sense anyway. It may be that the elements of astrology that could do this are not yet known or that the period is too long, though more to the point would be Jesus's words in Matthew 24:36. All of chapter 24 is pertinent from an end times perspective but this 36th verse is most relevant to our current question. Jesus has been asked by his disciples what will be the sign of the end of the age which would equate to the culminating point of the end times. He speaks of war, famine, and earthquakes but describes these as preliminary indications only. He then says that the *"gospel of the kingdom will be preached in all the world as a testimony to all nations, and then the end will come."* This, as a matter of interest, has now come to pass. Finally, Jesus tells his disciples, *"No one knows about that day or hour, not even the angels in heaven, nor the Son, but only the Father."*

No one knows, and no one will be able to predict. This is the implication. One might imagine that the end of the end times, as the tail of the Iron Age and the conclusion to an entire cycle, would be accompanied by various eclipses and oppositions of ill-matched planets, perhaps a comet or two, and some astrologers do regard the very close gathering together of the five visible planets plus the moon in Libra on September 8, 2040, as significant. However, what Jesus is saying is that it is a spiritual event known only by God, and this tells us that we should respond to it on a spiritual level. Astrology relates to the phenomenal world, using the word phenomenal in its widest sense to include the world of the psyche which is external to a true spiritual perspective. It is of great significance in that world, but it is not spiritually significant, which is not to disparage it but simply to put it in its proper place. We can be guided by it up to a point, but we must also go beyond it just as we must go beyond the Creation to know the Creator. And above all, the end times is the time for seeking to get to know the Creator. The dissolution of all that is good and right in the world that occurs then can help us to do this by forcing us to let go of our worldly attachments.

If we could really read the signs and patterns and movements in the heavens, we would know the secrets of the cosmos and those of the human heart because all is connected. At the same time, everything expresses the celestial archetypes according to its own nature, giving us the perfect balance between freedom and necessity. Nothing is rigidly determined by the stars, but all things respond to their influence, using conventional language to describe the process. And yet behind all this movement lies the stillness of eternity. The stars are like angels who are the messengers of God, and this is how we should see astrology. God speaks to us through the stars, but he himself as he is in himself is not to be found in the outer universe which he transcends in all its aspects, even the most majestic. Astrology relates to the gods but not to God except in his outer workings.

The Gnostic World View

Gnosticism has a bad reputation among Christians but there are elements of it that complement conventional religious understanding, and these can offer deeper insights into the spiritual life particularly in times like now when all formal religious structures are collapsing, with the light they contain going out and their salvific power much reduced. This is an expected phenomenon of the end times when forms disintegrate, quite literally lose their integrity, but is no less disconcerting for all that when you are obliged to live through it. You might say that official channels are being closed off so we look where we can for inspiration. However, when we do, we must be alert because in all esoteric spirituality, mixed in with the inspiration, there is also illusion and misdirection.

As far as Gnosticism is concerned, we can reject the idea of a Demiurge on a lower level of spiritual reality to the transcendent God who is responsible for the creation of the world with its inbuilt flaws. A basic truth is that God saw Creation and said that it was good. Matter is not evil, but it is matter and therefore a more constricted state of being than spirit. It is temporal and subject to decay, but it is not evil. The absolute duality of good and evil, spirit and matter, that exists in some versions of Gnosticism, most notably the Manichaean, is also based on a misconception. The world has fallen into darkness but darkness or evil has no separate reality independent of God.

Where some Gnostic ideas are useful is regarding the nature of the soul. For the conventional Christian, souls are made at conception or around that time. This is far from the case, and I would go so far as to say it is spiritually incoherent. The notion may have come about because the destiny and purpose of Western man was to focus more fully on the material plane than earlier cultures had done, with the aim of developing a more rounded and complete sense of an individual self. The idea that your real self was elsewhere or that you had many lives to develop your consciousness would potentially prevent the building up of a strong individuality and engaging fully with the material world, and this was the path laid out for Western man whose goal was to conquer matter after fully experiencing it.

Be that as it may, Gnosticism is correct when it says that souls exist on the spiritual level in realms of light from whence they come down to earth to experience life in a physical body and a sphere of being in which they have become separated from God. This is so that they may grow, become independent and, ultimately, if all goes well, return as fully functioning members of the Kingdom of Heaven. John 3:13 says, *"No man has ascended up to heaven, but he that came down from heaven."* The verse goes on to say, *"even the Son of man which is in heaven,"* and is normally understood as a reference to Jesus, but it can also be seen as referring to men as spiritual beings who incarnate in this world to further their evolution. The acorn falls from the oak into the darkness of the ground but then is drawn upwards, returning to the light as a fully formed tree having garnered the nutrients available in matter.

The Gnostic idea of man as a divine spark trapped in matter from which it must extricate itself is broadly correct. Where it errs is in not seeing this as intentional. There is purpose behind it. It is not simply that the soul has fallen into darkness and ignorance, but that it has come to this state to learn and grow. On its own level, the soul is perfect but relatively passive. It is bathed in unselfconscious bliss but with no chance to deepen its understanding or develop its creative capacities. To do this it must come to a world where it is thrown back on itself, faces challenges, experiences the full range of emotions and difficulties and problems that it must surmount through its own powers. This is the world of separation which is the material world.

However, things are not quite that simple because this world is not only material, that's to say, outside pure spirit; it has also fallen and so is worse than it might have been. This is where the Gnostic misunderstanding comes in. Yes, the world has been damaged. No, it is not on that account evil. Evil is nothing in itself. It can only inflict harm on good. Good is the reality, and evil is just the shadow of reality in a dualistic world of light and darkness. Darkness is not a thing. It is just the absence of light.

So, the soul comes down to earth with the aim of returning to the heavenly realm through a conscious choice by first identifying and then positively disidentifying with the material world and the vehicles it uses to interact with that world. This act of choosing qualifies the soul to go to a higher level than that from which it emanated but it also means there is an element of risk involved. It may make the wrong choice or not make the right one, not quite the same thing. And yet the risk is necessary because the soul must form itself by consciously allying itself with God and the principles of Creation. God makes the raw material, but the soul must then build itself up from that raw material if it is to be, which is the intention, a real individual and hence a potential god itself.

Gnosticism means knowledge. The soul is required to have spiritual knowledge. That much should be obvious, but which is more important, knowledge or faith? On a spiritual level, they are the same thing. It is only in worldly terms that they become separated and sometimes even exist in conflict, though that just means that they are both very imperfect in this world. The aim is to unite them and know them as two modes of the same spiritual faculty.

The Gnostic system may be flawed but it has many insights. Deriving from ideas received by way of ancient Iran and India, with teaching from Orpheus and Plato thrown in as well as Christianity, it is a ragbag of influences, but it mixes these together to make its own system. Its positive side is its vision of man as a shining spiritual being with a glorious destiny (if he will take it), while its defect is to regard the material world as evil. Christians would agree that the world is fallen and under the thumb of Satan, the so-called prince of this world, but it was created by God and is not a prison but a school of learning in which the soul may come to know itself through a process of externalisation, meaning growth through resolving the tension of a division between subject and object, which on its own plane it barely knows. The major Gnostic insight, that man is a spiritual being with his destiny in the stars, is one we need more than ever in these end times when all worldly solutions to the crises we are faced with will fail. The primary vision of Gnosticism centres on that fact of man as a being of light, and light is what the end times lack almost by definition. The notion that we are a spark of divine light in our essential being is something to hold onto in a time of spreading darkness and can counterbalance the unsatisfactory to the modern mind and, in some respects, inhuman attitude of traditional religion that we are sinners. So long as you understand that the one does not preclude the other, and that we are indeed sinners in terms of our worldly selves. Nevertheless, the deeper truth is that we come from light and to light we will return if that is what we wish. Every man is indeed, or has the potential to be, a star.

The Guru in the End Times

As the Iron Age reaches its latter stages, the receding of spirit and the dominance of the material pole lead to the dissolution of Form which, in turn, causes an erosion of boundaries, levelling of qualities, and hollowing out of structure. All institutions set up to serve and establish a culture lose contact with their core function and become self-serving.

The institution of the guru does not escape this process. Ideally, the guru is a wise teacher who can guide his disciples along the spiritual path but here, as elsewhere, the democratisation of an office has been followed by a loss of quality. The guru is a figure of Eastern spirituality, but the idea came West over the last century with, it must be said, very mixed results.

There is actually one area of Western spirituality where something like a guru does exist and that is Russian Orthodox Christianity. Before the communist revolution in Russia, a prospective monk became the pupil of a spiritual father rather like Alyosha and Father Zosima in *The Brothers Karamazov* by Dostoyevsky. The novice was required to obey his spiritual superior without question as a child should do to its parent. However, the revolution broke the chain of monastic tradition. The American Russian Orthodox priest Seraphim Rose, who was a man of genuine insight and saintliness of character, thought that the destruction wrought by the communists meant that the spiritual links between master to disciple could no longer be passed down. He associated this rupture with the end times, and thought it meant that henceforth obedience to the guru had to be replaced by personal discernment. The second half of the 20th century proved him right as thousands of seekers with more spiritual ambition than sense were led astray by unscrupulous popularisers and spiritual showmen unbacked by any real longstanding tradition.

One of the consequences of the end times is the retraction of the vertical pole, associated with spirit, and the expansion of the horizontal which is the material side. This produces more breadth but less depth, and applied to the sphere of spirituality means there will be a greater number of public teachers, but they have less to offer. Here is one example of how that worked out.

Alan Watts was a populariser of Buddhism, especially Zen Buddhism, in the 1950s, at a time when the appeal of Eastern religion was strong among a certain spiritually deracinated intellectual class. I first came across one of his books many years ago but only read a few pages before putting the book away. It was well-written and even insightful in part, but it was also obvious that here was someone who had the words off pat but didn't live the teachings except superficially. Reading something like that does more harm than good because, while it may feed the mind, its essential insincerity damages the soul if taken seriously. This apparently was Seraphim Rose's opinion too. He was attracted to Watts at first and became his student but soon saw through him. Film exists of Watts speaking to an audience and there you can see the typical tendency of the modern guru of seeking to project a magnetic personality in order to cast a spell on his audience.

And this is just what so many guru figures of recent decades have done. The glamour of being seen as the spiritually enlightened master is very strong, and charismatic figures are drawn to it as a way to feed their egos and dominate lesser mortals who give them energy through their devotion. These teachers cannot all be said to be evil (though some can), and they may do good at some level, but many use spirituality to advance themselves and don't care about their disciples other than as satellites revolving around their sun. Watts, like other prominent gurus and spiritual teachers of the last 100 years, taught a form of mysticism which promised spiritual benefits while allowing its adherents to do more or less what they wanted. His spiritual vision was tailored to cater to the modern taste for self-worship and hedonism.

And this is what happens when you take God and the idea of sin out of the equation. Then you use spirituality as a consumer product, a therapy, or simply as something to boost the self.

The change in human consciousness over the last 200 years, with its greater sense of individualism and freedom, means that the age of the guru is past. There is still a place for spiritual teachers of some description, but not for the guru as the supreme dispenser of wisdom and enlightenment who must be looked up to almost as though he were God or, at least, a god. That was never a Western concept anyway, but the guru became a romantic figure in the 20th century, and a number of unscrupulous spiritual salesmen hopped on board that train. Alan Watts was by no means the worst, but he was a definite type.

Moving on from the guru to spiritual teachers in general, and notwithstanding what I have just said, it is an unfortunate fact that in the end times most spiritual teachers are of little real use. Not long ago I was sent some advertising material for a prominent Mind, Body, and Spirit Festival. Many of the spiritual professionals who appear at affairs such as these in talks and workshops are really just businesspeople who have a talent for giving a presentation and who cater to those who seek spirituality as a lifestyle accessory or means to develop themselves. They are the psychics, intuitives, positive thinkers, motivational speakers, wellness experts, and aura readers who offer a kind of therapeutic self-help for people looking to expand their horizons a bit beyond the material world in a way that doesn't require much moral or intellectual repentance and sacrifice. You could say they are a stage to be gone through, but you don't need to experience that stage to realise its essential shallowness.

Probably many of these teachers believe they are doing good, and perhaps some of them are to a degree, but often they lead people away from true spiritual understanding down one of the many blind alleys that the novice might encounter when he first starts to aspire to something more than this world has to offer. Anybody who makes spirituality his profession, other than a bona fide priest who anyway follows a vocation not a profession and is certainly not in it for fame or fortune, is either a fraud or, since most of them are not that, an opportunist or, best case scenario, on a not very high rung of spiritual understanding and teaching half-truths that offer a spirituality intended to make one feel good. The spiritual path is not about making the earthly self feel happy or fulfilled or even loving and good. Its sole purpose is to reorient the heart and mind to God.

Are there no spiritual teachers worth following? It depends on what you mean by teacher. There are certainly people from whom one can learn but the whole concept of a spiritual teacher is foreign to the West. It is imported from Eastern religion, and therefore it is operating on a different sort of level. But even on that level the spiritual teacher role as it exists now exists as much for the teacher's sake as it does for the pupil. Certainly, we can and should share our understanding, but the spiritual path today is an individual path, and all teachers can do is give us a push in the right direction at an early stage. Thereafter, we must form our own relationship with God. No doubt many teachers would say exactly that but often by their behaviour they encourage dependence, personality worship, and idolatry. Nowadays the spiritual teacher is often just another manifestation of contemporary celebrity culture, and this, while it may always have existed to a certain extent, is a definite sign of the end times.

The notion of spiritual teachers who can transmit their understanding through their own realisation is connected to the increasingly redundant concept of New Age spirituality with its promiscuous mix of occultism, paganism, and a Western interpretation of Eastern religion, which are boiled down into a kind of 'oneness' spirituality that regards spirit as an impersonal energy source which can be tapped and used with the right technique. This can be regarded as spirituality for atheists in that it has no fundamental argument with either science or liberal ideology, which both derive from materialistic assumptions and fit alongside it with minimal discomfort. The problem here is that God is rejected except as a synonym for the universal cosmic force that is the same in us as it is throughout the universe. Hence, personhood as a real and fundamental thing is lost, and when personhood is lost so is love, and so also is the idea of personal responsibility or sin. The teachers of universal, impersonal spirituality cannot admit that love is superfluous to their system because love is central to any spiritual understanding *post* Jesus, and so they must perform metaphysical acrobatics to fit it in though the inconsistencies are rarely acknowledged. The same applies to matters of good and evil. In a world of oneness, good and evil must be seen as two branches of the same tree, and when that happens you fail to recognise evil, which means it can easily gain a purchase in your mind, disguising itself as a more enlightened understanding.

Human beings are spiritual beings and in a materialistic culture which denies spirit they will search for something that can satisfy an innate unsatisfied hunger. But most will not know where to look and will not be sufficiently discerning to recognise that between the material and the true spiritual there is a vast hinterland of being that is neither one nor the other but can seem to partake of elements of both. This is the world of myth and fairy tale, and imagination and dreams, and gods and demons, and all manner of psychic phenomena, good, bad, and indifferent. It can nourish or it can harm, and it is where the great majority of modern-day end times spiritual teachers reside in terms of consciousness. But it is not where God and his saints are to be found.

Jesus Was a Refugee

Or so it is sometimes said, but was he really or is this just used as a way of disarming objections to the globalist project of breaking down national identities so that humanity can be herded into a system of collectivist control? Setting aside the fact that Jesus only went from one part of the Roman Empire to another, a close neighbour, he and his family were refugees for a relatively brief period when they moved to escape King Herod. But they would not have received any financial assistance from that country, nor would they have had a say in how it was run. Furthermore, they returned to their own country as soon as they could. The Holy Family's situation was not parallel to that of refugees today which point I only make to show the weakness of the Jesus was a refugee argument made by those who seem to think it can be applied to anyone who claims refugee status today, and used in the broader sense to justify the modern phenomenon of mass immigration.

Mass immigration inevitably destroys a country as a unified form. The physical entity will remain, a society of some sort will endure, but it will be nothing like the country that existed before. That is gone. You might say time changes a country anyway, but there is organic change and then there is complete revolution. One is growth but the other is replacement. Mass immigration is replacement. There are no two ways about this. I was brought up in London. The city now is a totally different place with totally different people. Obviously, times change but this is not change. It is radical transformation. You might say this is not a bad thing. It just is what it is. However, the fact remains that London and its people as they were for a very long time, the ones who actually built the place, have gone.

People emigrate to a country because they think they will have a better life there, but human beings are not all the same, and people who made the better off country are likely to have certain qualities that others do not have or not to the same degree. That means that any country that undergoes mass immigration will sooner or later start to resemble those usually more backward countries from which the immigrants came. This may not be inevitable if the newcomers can be properly integrated but the whole point of mass immigration, such as almost all Western countries have experienced over the last 2 to 3 decades, is that the excessively large number means they cannot be assimilated. Then trust between the various communities diminishes to the point that social cohesion starts to dissolve, and the sense of national identity is lost. You have various groups fighting for power and with very different end goals.

In Matthew chapter 25 Jesus tells us a parable about the sheep and the goats. He relates how the righteous will be rewarded for their good deeds on Earth. These include feeding him when he was hungry and looking after him when he was sick. When those so commended are puzzled about this he tells them that what they did for the least of his brothers they did for him. Note that word. Brothers. There is no suggestion that this has a universal application. It surely refers to those who share Jesus's vision of life and whose hearts are set on the Kingdom of Heaven as opposed to this world. Your spiritual brother is not every other human being, regardless of what he believes and his attitude to life, but those human beings who acknowledge and accept God. This doesn't mean you shouldn't help others when you can, but nor does it mean that a nation is spiritually obliged to have an open-door policy. Besides which, personal morality and national policy are not and should not be the same thing. And after all, isn't loving your neighbour primarily to do with loving your neighbour? Mass immigration by its effect on a country is very likely to harm many of your real neighbours, i.e. fellow countrymen and women, in the sense of putting pressure on house prices, welfare, education, and health budgets, and many other aspects of life not to mention the general culture and sense of nationhood. There is a glib, sentimental morality that just looks to the obvious and the immediately pleasing, and there is a more mature and spiritually balanced morality that looks at the wider picture and considers the deeper ramifications of a particular act.

The fact is that mass immigration has been used as a specific tool, one of several but a significant one, to destroy the West. The West must be destroyed because its civilisation and culture were grounded in Christianity. To that end compassion has been weaponised and turned against itself. I have to say that only the naive and those of bad faith are duped by this, but there are a lot of them especially in the intellectual classes. These people want to feel morally superior and so they adopt certain attitudes that will help them do so. They also live in the world of abstract theory as opposed to reality and thus are easy victims of ideological propaganda, which a simpler mindset would see through because it clashes with everyday reality.

Many church leaders criticise those who point to the errors of mass immigration. They may mean well, a perennial excuse for lack of imagination, but what does it mean to mean well? Does it mean they are doing what they think is right or Christian? What if they don't know what is right or, indeed, Christian? Their Christianity is heavily mixed up with Enlightenment humanism which was a specific rejection of supernatural Christianity and promoted its social aspect, its least important aspect, to become not just the totality of moral understanding but also to a universal plane. The church leaders may have good intentions according to their limited grasp of spiritual reality, but their morality is grounded in Enlightenment humanism not the teachings of Christ. They are materialists, religious administrators whose task is to conform religion to worldly society, and who speak for man not God as is only to be expected in an end times period.

The modern world doesn't like boundaries, but God does. God has created very strict boundaries between spirit and matter, between heaven and hell, and also between the various levels of the higher worlds to which you can only ascend when spiritually qualified to do so. This does not mean that boundaries should never be crossed but nor should they be totally disregarded. There is no form without boundaries. Boundaries define and they protect, and good things need protection in a world in which the darkness is constantly trying to overcome the light.

I am not against immigration *per se* but, like everything, it depends on time and place. It is sometimes right and often wrong, depending on circumstances. A country's first responsibility is to the people who live there, its own group. Certainly, if it can, it should extend a welcome to others who may be persecuted in their own lands, but this cannot be an endless process or the nation will effectively be committing suicide. The Bible says we should welcome the stranger by which it means we should treat strangers well during their visit. It doesn't say that they should stay forever, and nor does it say you should carry on welcoming strangers until you have destroyed your own nation. Yet this is the disastrous path the West is set upon in the end times, one of the distinguishing characteristics of which is precisely this dissolution of borders and homogenisation of quality. That may be happening anyway, but it is also being exploited by certain forces that seek to erode national identity not for a higher spiritual end, but to establish an easily controllable collective. And behind even those there are powers looking to make negative spiritual capital out of the likely conflict that will arise as it always has in the past when something similar has been attempted though it never has on the current scale.

The Wisdom of the Left

It's a contradiction in terms, isn't it? Can a left-wing person or principle ever be thought of as wise? It just doesn't fit, and the reason it doesn't is that leftism is a secular ideology. Wisdom is of necessity a spiritual thing. It must be as it goes beyond logic, reason and, particularly, ideology. We may talk about the wisdom of crowds but that is a misuse of the word. It simply means a kind of natural instinct. Even the wisdom of age is just knowledge gleaned from experience. But true wisdom is perception into the heart of spiritual reality, and it cannot be associated with leftism which only relates to political, social, or economic matters, in other words, to worldliness. These days there exist many spiritual and religious people with leftist views, but this represents an inconsistency on their part, an inability to understand the reality of spirit. They are victims of the end times' dominance of materialistic thought which has contaminated their spiritual perception. It's rather like serving God and Mammon. One of them must fall by the wayside. A spiritual leftist will always have one foot in this world. He is always grafting his spirituality onto his worldliness rather than taking everything from true spiritual perception.

This is not to say that the political right is in any respect wise, but here's the difference. Left and Right in their origins are not complementary opposites. Leftism is an ideology which has the supposed goal of leading humanity to a worldly utopia through societal reconstruction. It is based on theory and abstract reasoning, and it assumes (without any evidence) that human beings are fundamentally good. The Right, on the other hand, is the traditional way of dealing with reality with all its irregularities and flaws, as it is not as it ought to be. The Right, which in its modern form is deeply compromised and has accommodated itself to leftist thought in many areas, may not be wise as such but wisdom accepts the primacy of the spiritual world, and leftism arose as a specific rejection of that while the right, before it became secularised and largely captured by money, was grounded in the acknowledgement of God, and some of that remains, albeit heavily diluted. Wisdom is neither left nor right, but leftist principles are a categorical denial of wisdom which is based in the reality of God which means God as he is, not as reimagined by secular humanism in a form more congenial to itself.

Another point I would make to support this argument is that wisdom is hierarchical whereas leftism is egalitarian. That is almost its defining principle. It leaves out the transcendent, but wisdom derives from knowledge of transcendental reality. The transcendent is the vertical pole of being which is the primary pole, the horizontal only coming about when one becomes two in manifestation. And although the transcendent in itself is above hierarchy, when it manifests in creation it does so through hierarchical structure which stretches from the depths of matter or primeval chaos to the heights of spirit and perfect order.

Egalitarianism is linked in the modern mind to the idea of oneness but, again showing end times influence, this egalitarian oneness is that of matter, ultimately prime matter in which all quality is dissolved into no quality or cosmic mush. Creation brings about difference, and its movement through time brings greater expression, which is more difference. The oneness of egalitarianism is an anti-spiritual oneness for it takes us back to the primeval waters before they were touched by the Spirit of God. True spiritual oneness incorporates difference, it does not eradicate it, and if you are looking for a reason for creation then this is it. Which is better, a painting or a blank canvas?

The confusion here is that the spiritual goal is misconceived. The idea is not to overcome difference through regression to the non-separateness of pre-conscious existence, but to grow from unconscious oneness to conscious union, aligning personal identity with the Supreme Identity of the living God.

I include this chapter under the Spiritual Tradition heading because the left represents anti-tradition. That does not mean it has nothing to offer, but it only addresses a small fraction of human reality and, by dismissing the greater part of life, might reasonably be said, in contrast to how it presents itself, to be an anti-human philosophy. It lacks and can never have wisdom and therefore it only touches the most superficial level of human experience, and appeals to the most basic desires and ambitions of the human soul. Let's not even go into the fact that much of the leftist impulse arises from resentment and desire for power. Some people claim that the legitimate concerns that are manifested in leftism grew out of Christianity, but egalitarian ideals only emerged as Christianity lost its spiritual force and began to be interpreted on a social level. It is therefore what is left as the spiritual element of the religion, which is its raison d'être, is lost. The impulse to egalitarianism might be said to derive from the valuing of each individual soul which is a Christian concept, but it is a reduction of this idea to the material plane and an obvious distortion of it. Like all false ideas, its inherent inconsistencies become clear when it bumps up against reality, but those who take it as an article of faith or make it their religion will refuse to recognise that fact. What might seem to give them some justification is that, in a way, they are right. If you take the essence of egalitarianism as saying that all human beings have intrinsic dignity, then it is true. If you say that all human beings deserve justice and fair treatment that is also true. But human beings are not all the same and nor is it God's purpose to make them all the same. The drive towards egalitarianism may be understandable as a reaction against oppression and the denial of individual worth, but it can only serve as a stepping stone to deeper understanding for as it stands it is a false and spiritually destructive doctrine. Advocates might point to early human societies that were supposedly equal but even if that were the case, and more recent research has cast doubt on it, to revert to a pre-conscious state would be like a flower returning from bloom to bud. The way forward is to incorporate the fruits of evolutionary development and to build on them, not to retreat to spiritual childhood.

Who Is Sophia? What Is She?

Modernity was born out of the Reformation. Nothing starts from nothing, and one can trace its antecedents a long way further back than that, but the Reformation was the manifestation in the religious domain, which up to that point had always been the primary domain, of the new consciousness, one with a greater focus on self, the rational mind, and the merely human. It was a step forward because it increased our powers of agency and self-determination. It moved us on to an increasingly active mode of participation in the world. This brought many advantages but also problems because human beings, first in the vanguard and then more or less everyone, were no longer directed by an external authority rooted in the real (cf. the instinctive nature of the animal kingdom), but by their own selves and those selves were, and still are, limited by and to the phenomenal world of sensory experience, though for some pioneering individuals journeys into the realm of abstract thought became possible. However, even these were restricted by the nature of thought centred on itself. Greater freedom and creativity became open to us, but the price was the loss of connection to everything that is summed up in the word 'God'. Our horizons became extended, but our vision contracted. You might say we saw further along the East/West axis but, as a result, the North/South axis collapsed. And yet this was necessary if we were to advance from the state of a being embedded in creation to one able to move out of that and manipulate creation ourselves. This was once again eating from the tree of knowledge of good and evil, and meant we could potentially become gods if we did this with due recognition of the will of God and in line with his natural and spiritual order, but, failing that and acting according to our own will, we might become devils.

With the Reformation and its rejection of authority the seeds were sown for every man to become his own pope. Eventually every man should be his own pope, but the pope is subject to God, and if every man becomes not his own pope but his own god then you have crossed the line from saint to demon. That line can sometimes be thin, and it does seem that humanity has not succeeded in avoiding it at the present time. We are called to be individual but not to be individualistic. Our destiny is to be gods in creation, able in the fullness of time to create worlds ourselves, but never to be our own gods. A god must serve the will of God or he becomes a devil.

The Protestant Reformation created the modern world which is why the main drivers of modernity until its corruption were those countries in which that ethos was most fully embedded. The spirit of the times was everywhere and that spirit created outcomes in most places, but still the Protestant countries were at the centre of it all. One of the defining characteristics of Protestantism was its rejection, either overtly or in effect, of the supernatural. While this meant it could focus its energies more fully on the material plane as was intended by the powers that be, for the short term anyway, it also resulted in it becoming spiritually dry and unfulfilling. Religion without the supernatural becomes legalistic and limited to morality. It has no real life or colour or joy or mystery or power to uplift and inspire. It's an arranged marriage rather than one founded on love. In line with this, Protestantism also demoted the Mother of God to just a human being. It lost touch with the Divine Feminine.

When the Romantic movement arose at the end of the 18th century as a reaction fuelled by the reassertion of imagination against the dry rationalistic spirit of the Enlightenment, poets, artists, writers, and philosophers rediscovered the Divine Feminine. How best to define this elusive term? Perhaps by identifying it with the soul of things just as God the Father is identified with the spirit. As such it is linked to beauty, mystery, and love in contrast to will, life, and being. It is also associated with wisdom, and in this aspect the Divine Feminine is identified as Sophia.

In the Western canon Sophia is the Divine Feminine in her most elevated mode of being. According to some she actually incarnated in the Virgin Mary just as the second person of the Trinity did in Jesus. A debate has long been going on about whether she is created or uncreated with some enthusiasts equating her with the Holy Spirit, the third person of the Trinity. This might seem to have a certain logic to it were it not for the fact that it contradicts scripture which describes her as a created feminine image of God. The very first created being but still a created being. In beautiful language chapter 8 of Proverbs extols her thus:

The Lord brought me forth as the first of his works before his deeds of old;
I was formed long ages ago, at the very beginning, when the world came to be.
When there were no watery depths, I was given birth, when there were no springs overflowing with water;
before the mountains were settled in place, before the hills, I was given birth,
before he made the world or its fields or any of the dust of the earth.
I was there when he set the heavens in place, when he marked out the horizon on the face of the deep,
when he established the clouds above and fixed securely the fountains of the deep,
when he gave the sea its boundary so the waters would not overstep his command, and when he marked out the foundations of the earth.
Then I was constantly at his side. I was filled with delight day after day, rejoicing always in his presence,
rejoicing in his whole world and delighting in mankind.

The apocryphal Book of Wisdom in chapter 7 supports this when it says of Sophia that:

> *She is a breath of the power of God, and a pure emanation of the glory of the Almighty; therefore nothing defiled gains entrance into her. For she is a reflection of eternal light, a spotless mirror of the working of God, and an image of his goodness.*

These Old Testament quotes can be taken as authoritative or not. They certainly have a poetic truth. However, part of the modern mindset when applied to the spiritual quest is that nothing can be taken as unquestionable just on say so. We must always use our own intelligence and intuition though making sure it is intuition and not personal preference or preconception. The Divine Feminine is an important part of spiritual reality but associating her with the third person of the Trinity goes against the fundamental Christian teaching that Mary, who is, actually or symbolically, the embodiment of Sophia and the Divine Feminine, conceived Jesus by power of the Holy Spirit. It is to also to misunderstand the nature of spirit and project worldly prejudices onto spiritual reality.

One can see why the Protestant suppression of the Divine Feminine might cause her to reappear in unbalanced or exaggerated forms, action and reaction being equal and opposite and all that, but still, one should know that there is a feminine dimension to divine reality without going to the extreme of feminising God as making the Holy Spirit feminine does. Seeing Sophia as the first of the Lord's works gives us an insight as to where the Divine Feminine might arise, but she is not just the first created being. She is the actual foundation principle or Matrix of creation. As substance and even space she is the Universal Mother and World Soul, the *prima materia* who receives the image of God and who ultimately becomes the Heavenly Bride or Divine

Spouse. She as the Feminine principle must arise before anything can be created because everything is created out of her body.

Going back to her source, she can be envisaged as arising from the receptive nature of God which comes into being when the positive principle of pure act takes expression as its complementary opposite, creation necessarily being founded on duality since a world of subject alone would be unknowable. You cannot say she comes after the male principle in terms of time since the two in their manifested forms must arise together as one suggests the other, but in this Spirit/Matter or Subject/Object complementary duo one is ontologically prior to the other. Thus, as Wisdom says, she is a reflection of God once God moves into his polarised mode of creativity from his original uncreated form, the hidden God which is behind and beyond everything. This is why she is, as Mary her incarnation in human form says, submissive to God. Her will is to do his will not the other way around for although the two arise together in time, they arise out of his pre-temporal being.

I think this insight might resolve a difficulty with feminist spirituality which is right to see the feminine as integral to divine reality, there from the beginning, but fails to see there is a hierarchical distinction. Sophia is the first of everything in Creation, but she still comes from God the Father who is the Creator. In Christian terms she would be the *Nihil* from which God creates, but there is no nothing and that just means she comes from him.

From God the Creator comes Sophia who is the light and glory of the Father, arising when he expresses himself in creation. She is the mirror in which he sees himself. She becomes his Consort and in a certain sense includes the whole of creation in herself as it is in relation to God. At the end of days when all is accomplished, she will sit in glory alongside him on his heavenly throne, created by God out of himself and now through his great love raised up to be his height.

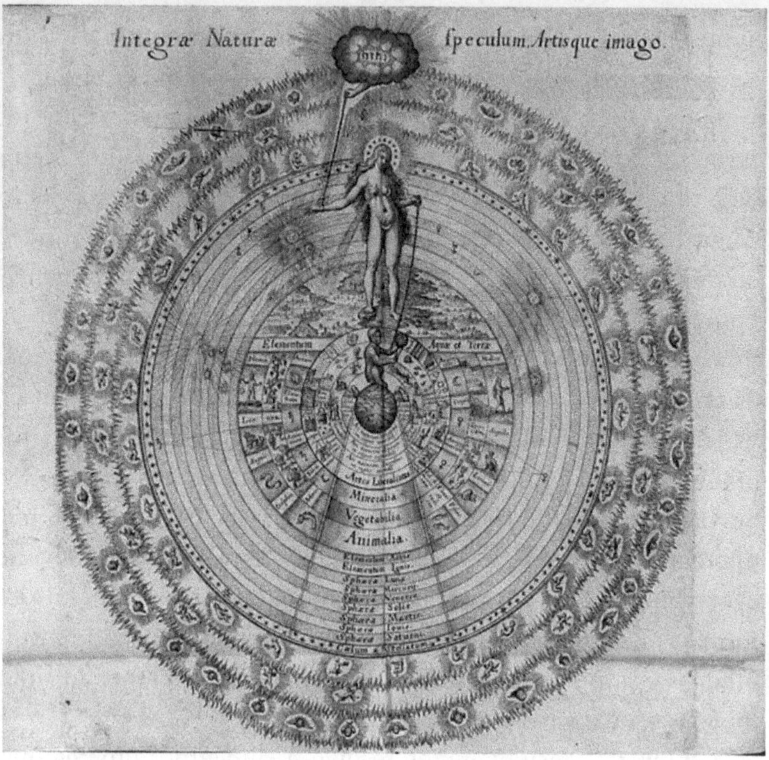

I have used this image in a previous book but here it is again because it conveys so much. It comes from Robert Fludd's *Utriusque Cosmi*, or History of the Two Worlds (Macrocosm and Microcosm), and can be interpreted in various ways. In the context of our current theme, it shows Sophia as Queen of Creation. She presides over all the created worlds, outer and inner, shown by the concentric circles, but is linked by the chain attached to her right hand to the hand of God who is hidden in the cloud above the circle of angels. The image shows the relationship of God to Sophia and Sophia to the universe. He is the Creator, she the Creation which is formed by him from her body.

The Tree of Knowledge of Good and Evil

The story of creation and Adam and Eve in the Garden of Eden as told in the first three chapters of the book of Genesis is one of the most interesting spiritual texts that has come down to us. For here, told in the simplest of terms, is the story of how we were created and why we are as we are now. The story has different elements to it and can be taken on different levels, but the aspect I want to look at here concerns the tree of knowledge of good and evil.

Here's the relevant passage:

> *And the Lord God commanded the man, "You may freely eat of every tree of the garden; but of the tree of the knowledge of good and evil you shall not eat, for in the day you eat of it you shall die."*

The first thing to note is that this is all in Paradise and so this tree forms part of Paradise. Everything in Paradise has been created by God and everything there is good, so the tree in itself is good. What is the tree and what is its fruit? The tree is knowledge of good and evil or just knowledge so clearly the tree is the self-conscious mind and the fruit is that which awakens mind, thought. Adam and Eve did not have an awakened mind before eating the fruit. Thereafter, their eyes were opened which means their mind, their capacity for self-reflection and thought, awoke.

Does this mean the serpent was correct and Adam and Eve were right to listen to him? After all, they moved out of naive innocence into a world of experience in which they could grow. In the prelapsarian Garden of Eden nothing could change or so it might seem. This is a theory certain esoteric schools would subscribe to and they would see the serpent/Lucifer as the Light

Bearer his name implies, being either a liberator of humanity in a Promethean sense, freeing us from a tyrannical Gnostic-type Archon god, or else simply working in line with the needs of evolutionary development by helping to awaken mind in infant humanity who were little more than animal men at that stage.

In my view this ostensibly reasonable scenario is a misdirection, plausible on the surface but quite wrong on deeper investigation. We know that God is love and God is good. As in goodness is God – there is no goodness apart from God. God is also truth so what he says about not eating the fruit from the tree of knowledge of good and evil is also truth. And yet it awoke mind in man so how do we reconcile these two facts? The fruit is knowledge, and knowledge is essentially good but there are two sorts of knowledge. The knowledge that comes from God and the knowledge that comes from self. Eating the fruit from the tree after having been told not to do this gave knowledge apart from God. It was the act of a being that wished to become a god itself without reference to the true God. One can speculate that the fruit was not in itself evil but eating it before being ready to do so, and after having been specifically told not to, made it the source of sin and death.

Knowledge is good. As potential co-creators with God we are called to knowledge, but that knowledge should be centred in an awareness of the full reality and purpose of God. Knowledge without that acceptance becomes evil, or there is the strong likelihood it will become so. The serpent tempted Eve to disobey God and so deny her Creator and assert the separate self. He also prompted her to go against Adam, again appealing to ego. This was the cause of evil and why Lucifer is no heroic freedom fighter but a rebel against goodness and truth, something that continues to this day.

The Garden of Eden was a spiritual nursery, and the point of a nursery is to nurture. To protect immature consciousness as it grows. It is like a buffer state between the womb and the world. In this case, the womb is the realm of oneness, of non-separation, and the world is the world of duality, of subject and object, the self and everything else, a world in which growth may be possible as it is not in oneness where there is no challenge to bring it forth. Evil existed in the universe at the time of the Garden, having come into active being with the Fall of Lucifer and the angels, which is a myth that expresses a reality. The presence of the serpent in the Garden confirms that sad fact. However, it did not yet exist for infant humanity which lived and thought naturally, according to a pattern laid down by the Creator. What did exist was freedom which necessarily includes the potential to go wrong or off-piste as one might say. One may speculate that Eve was glamoured by the allure of being a queen, and it was on an incipient vanity that the serpent played. Something similar is expressed in the Greek myth of Narcissus of whom it was prophesied that he would live as long as he did not know himself. The bite of the apple caused Adam and Eve to know themselves for the first time which means that they fell into separation because they experienced full self-consciousness before they were spiritually mature enough to deal with it. Self-consciousness was their destiny but in God's time when they were ready for it. The premature awareness of self caused the full identification with it which led to selfishness and all the evils of egotism. These are the risks of freedom.

In a sense, the end times is the coming to a head of that bite of the apple. They represent the cumulative effect of thousands, maybe tens or even hundreds of thousands, of years of wrong thinking and wrong action. They bring these to the surface, but they are also caused by them because if the Fall had never taken place, while there would still have been a fading of spirit and a strengthening of matter over time, that would have happened naturally so it would not have dragged consciousness down with it. Human unfoldment would have proceeded without the full extent of sin, darkness, and death because matter would always have been open to spirit instead of increasingly closed to it. Eating from the tree of knowledge of good and evil means there will be evil, and one of the spiritual meanings of the end times is the cleansing of evil through the full experience of it.

God created humanity so that beings other than himself might add to creation, perhaps in ways sometimes surprising even to him. That might sound naive but is why he bestowed free will on his creation. We were created to contribute our personal tone to the heavenly choir but to sing according to the rules of the eternal songbook of love and light. With the fall we sang out of tune with the whole, from our own songbook, according to our own self-made rules, thereby causing disharmony which led to discord which is sin, and we have been doing that ever since. Instead of following God which, let me repeat, is the same as the good, we followed our own egos in the attempt to become gods ourselves. Or not gods because that was and remains our destiny, but like God, a centre unto ourself. Jesus came to right that wrong and put us back on track. We had separated ourselves from our Maker through rebellion and seeking to become gods after our own pattern, but in Christ we are given the opportunity to attain a true union with God which will indeed make us godlike though now in the right way not the corrupted way offered by Satan in the Garden.

The end times see most of us still following the path of separation and self-advancement. We seem to be coming to some sort of crisis point as we pursue this path relentlessly while knowing it will lead to disaster, but what else can we do? Our culture, our ideologies, our obsession with material and social progress and, especially, our technologies all separate us from God, and although we consider ourselves to be rational and free we are, in fact, ever more the dupes of the serpent, the less we claim to believe in him. We are still eating fruit from that tree.

Tradition and Technology

One of the clearest indications that we live in the end times is the dominance of technology in our lives. For almost everyone, rich or poor, life is unthinkable without it. Modern technology is a very successful attempt to wrest control over matter but, paradoxically, that very success results in the increased control of matter over mind. The more we dominate matter, the more it dominates us. The fact that the technological separates us from the natural, never mind the spiritual, means that it is not just the material to which we are in thrall but the artificial as well, the artificial being that aspect of the material which is at the furthest remove from spirit. If the function of matter is to reflect and manifest spirit, then the artificial is matter which can no longer do that. It is the material severed from the spiritual which is exactly what the end times are all about. Nowadays, we do not just live in a materialistic age. We live in an artificial age.

I am writing this on a computer, and you may be reading it on one too. In the course of your work, you are probably using a computer for much of the time and, increasingly, your leisure hours will be spent looking at some form of computer. It is hard to imagine life today without these machines which have conquered the world in an incredibly short space of time. Many people may have reservations about certain aspects of the computer revolution but most still regard it as something whose advantages greatly outweigh its drawbacks. Here I'd like to argue the case that the computer and the technology associated with it are inherently anti-spiritual.

Of course, I'm not blind to the computer's many benefits, the ease of access to a seemingly limitless range of information, the speed of communication, the bringing together of physically separated like-minded individuals and so on. The computer would never have made such an impact if it had not opened up so many new opportunities, and there is no doubt that it has done so in virtually every field. All that is obvious. Yet there is a price to pay. I am reminded of Jesus's remark in Matthew 16:26: *"For what will it profit a man if he gains the whole world but loses his soul?"* I realise that puts me in the corner marked for cranks, killjoys, and Luddites, but I am not saying we should throw away our computers just yet. Only that we should be alive to the threat they represent. They are a fact of the modern world but that shouldn't mean we close our eyes to the dangers that come with them.

How is it that computers could cause you to lose your soul? Perhaps not literally, but what you lose is awareness of your soul so it amounts to the same thing. As you are caught up and absorbed in a virtual reality, so you become more disconnected from your soul. The outer takes over from the inner. The computer denatures life. It is the most significant advance yet of the machine and, as such, it points to the mechanisation of consciousness. It is that which will cause you to lose touch with your soul. The more you succumb to the lure of a computerised world, the more you lose the connection to the mystery of the world that lies beyond form and quantity which is the world of materialistic science.

Advocates of modern technology like to say that in itself it is neutral. It is what you do with it that raises questions, moral questions, questions of philosophy, and so on. They are mistaken. The acceptance of the dominance of technology in our lives is a psychological attitude, and what that attitude indicates is an implicit belief in the superiority of the mechanical over the natural. For the truth is the technology we use is neither neutral nor merely a means to an end which we may determine ourselves. It becomes an end, and that end as far as modern technology is concerned is the denaturing of the world leading to the separation of man from God.

You may consider this excessive but, as we have been told, you cannot serve God and Mammon. Mammon is not just money. It represents everything that is of this world, and what else is technology, the attempt to conquer nature by mechanical means, if not a thing of this world? This is not an argument for a return to the Stone Age, or even before that time since Stone Age man had axes and such like, but for a proper understanding of what modern technology actually is. Some form of technology has existed since *homo habilis,* the archaic human species from two million years ago, but each century since the 17th has seen material technology start to encroach on and then replace the spiritual though it can only do so in a parodic form.

I write this with no hope of appealing to anyone except the already converted, and with the full expectation that most people will reject it as nonsense. I would expect to be reminded of the countless lives that technology has saved, and I obviously don't dismiss that as insignificant though I would say that we all still die sooner or later, and our state of mind at death is more important than how long we live. We live forever anyway. No, the many benefits of modern technology are undeniable. But they are material benefits and cannot mask our utter dependence on it or that it robs us of the ability to respond to the soul. That means that our capacity to respond to real truth and real beauty, even real love, is much diminished. We are fobbed off with imitations and distortions of these things, and many of us don't notice though many do, even if only subliminally, resulting in feelings of discontent and pointlessness.

Perhaps this must be as anything that can be must eventually work itself out into the external world, and the end times would be the time for all that is hidden to come to the surface. That doesn't mean it is something to be embraced and regarded without circumspection because, even if it is inevitable, it may also represent a test for humanity to hold fast to a higher truth in the face of a sustained assault on the very notion of any such thing as higher truth. One of the tasks of all those who value the spiritual is to call the world back to its source, to point out that it has lost its way and been bewitched by the spurious glamour of fake gold. Fake gold is everywhere in the end times and the only way to avoid being corrupted by its alluring sparkle is to see beyond appearance and hold fast to purity.

The computer may just be a tool but our minds tend to reflect the technologies they use, and the limitations of these technologies become our own.

The latest manifestation of computer technology is AI, which is the fullest denial so far of spirit. It is humanity rejecting the reality of soul and farming out its consciousness to the machine. This is the modern cult of death in its grimmest form to date because it is a renunciation of both individuality and freedom. Neither can exist in a computer, and the more we embrace this technology the more we lose connection to what makes us human.

When will we learn that just because we can do something doesn't mean we should? There is the usual fake debate in which we question the use of AI and wonder if the robots will take over and destroy humanity, but we will still go ahead and everyone will jump on board just as they did with computers and smartphones. The machine will have made further inroads into our consciousness, and we will have put an even greater gulf between us and the reality of spirit. This is part of the ongoing descent into a world of pure quantity in which nothing exists that cannot be measured. Human creativity will be put in a box with its lid firmly fastened. We will be told that AI and creativity can run alongside each other, but it doesn't work like that. You either acknowledge the reality of spirit in which case AI will be recognised as anti-spirit or you ignore it in which case you enter a world in which everything is counted, controlled, numbered, and known. That is a form of death because it denies freedom which is life.

Then we have transhumanism which presents itself as a bright and shiny new development for humanity having the potential to bring enlightenment and immortality by manipulating our minds and bodies so that the errors and deficiencies of nature are corrected. This could be through mechanical, chemical, or biological means, but is essentially an artificial reconstruction based on purely materialistic methods. It sometimes claims a certain spiritual content but let's not forget that Satan is a spiritual being. His sin is not the denial of the spiritual so much as the denial of God. He approves of the spiritual as long as he can pervert it. Transhumanists have claimed in all seriousness that they are building God. No, they are not. They are building hell on earth. They are rejecting the true God and attempting to build a false one. A man-made one, an idol, which would turn out to be, if it ever came to pass, another means for the demonic powers to milk human energy and consciousness, which they need to do to survive and prosper, having cut themselves off from God. We would go into it expecting salvation, but it would really be damnation. Transhumanism is all about handing your soul over to the demons. It's the ultimate Faustian pact. You get power of some kind, though it's never what you really hoped for, but at the cost of your soul.

The transhumanists think they are pioneers in opening up consciousness and finding new ways of reconfiguring the human form while all the time they are following the oldest of paths that goes right back to the book of Genesis and Atlantean times. What Satan offered in the Garden of Eden was the transhumanist ticket. Be a god yourself. Forget God. The Tower of Babel was a transhumanist construction. Get to heaven without God. Be your own god. This is pure Satanism, and it leads to hell.

In the 1980s there were many people who identified with New Age types of spirituality who believed that computer technology was inspired by the spiritual powers. They thought the worldwide connectivity of the Internet was a forerunner of global consciousness, not realising that this technology was a parody of true spiritual understanding, Satan aping God as he likes to do but doing so in a crude and materialistic way since he is unable to do otherwise. As time has gone by, the possibility arises that modern computer technology may have been, to put it bluntly, demonically inspired, if not in its origin, then certainly in its development and use. How can it be otherwise since it substitutes the exterior for the interior and makes everything less real not more?

Computers reduce quality to quantity. That is the basis of their operations and, not coincidently, a defining characteristic of the end times. They are wholly materialistic in conception and function, but the effect of computers is spuriously spiritual in that they give theoretical access to all knowledge and have the capacity to simulate reality on a virtual level. The regular use of computers takes human beings away from their source and renders our thinking mechanical because the technologies we use coerce our minds into adopting the mindset which created them. This is certainly the case with computers.

If the IT revolution is demonically inspired, the question is why? The immediate answer might be to distract people from the spiritual and make them more susceptible to evil using that word in its broadest sense to mean anti-spiritual. Not just conventionally bad but wrong, that which separates us from truth. Computers are seductive and create a world of glamour and enchantment that allures us. They lead us away from nature into dreams and artificiality.

But is there more? It seems to be the case that the demons cannot take physical form except under certain very particular circumstances and for brief periods. UFO phenomena indicate that and stories from tradition about otherworldly beings inhabiting a kind of borderland between this world and the next say the same thing. Demons would probably like to incarnate directly on Earth because this would give them greater power over us. There might also be something about being in a body that they covet. Might the drive towards artificial intelligence, quantum computing and developing computers that are carbon-based actually be all about enabling demons to incarnate? C.S. Lewis explored ideas along these lines in his novel *That Hideous Strength* where the 'Macrobes' sought a kind of embodiment through the severed head of an executed evil genius type.

Many people are aware of the problems associated with humanity's addiction to IT. These are mostly to do with how it denatures us and reduces our ability to respond to the real world, never mind the spiritual world, properly. The increase in global surveillance is also a concern. But what if the true purpose of the computer revolution, the end game so to speak, was to enable the incarnation of demons in this world? This is a possibility we should start taking seriously.

Setting that aside, there is a passage in the book of Revelation which can be taken as referring to the outcome of this form of technology without too much stretching of the imagination.

> *And another angel, a third, followed them, saying with a loud voice, "If anyone worships the beast and its image and receives a mark on his forehead or on his hand, he also will drink the wine of God's wrath, poured full strength into the cup of his anger, and he will be tormented with fire and sulphur in the presence of the holy angels and in the presence of the Lamb. And the smoke of their torment goes up forever and ever, and they have no rest, day or night, these worshippers of the beast and its image, and whoever receives the mark of its name."* (Revelation 14:9–11)

Let's consider what this might mean in relation to computer technology. The use of it is not sinful as such though it can undoubtedly open the door to all sorts of temptations and distractions. Nonetheless, worshipping the beast and receiving the mark must entail more than simply using a computer or smartphone.

The devil is not a fool. He works in stages, leading us from seemingly innocent pursuits and preoccupations more and more deeply into his net until we end up doing and thinking and feeling things we never would have done when we started. So, once we have become so addicted to our smartphones that we cannot imagine life without them he will introduce another level and then another and so on, until there will finally come a point at which we will be led to make a conscious decision as to whether to carry on down this path or turn back. Carrying on will, in some way, mean renouncing God and rejecting spiritual truth.

Perhaps by then we will only be able to engage in any kind of economic activity if we allow ourselves to receive some kind of 'tag', even an implant, to get which we might have to take an oath of commitment to something that, in effect, denies God. Things do seem to be tending in that direction. The time may come when we have to choose whether to continue receiving our habitual worldly benefits, or maybe receive even greater benefits which we might not be aware of now but which will seem very attractive then, or not, and if we wish to get these things then we may have to do something similar to swearing allegiance to the old Roman gods, only something far more serious in its implications because it will require not just an outer gesture as that did but a real inner act of submission. By then the establishment hierarchy will probably be devil worshippers of some sort. (Some of them may already be that.) Though this elite will seem sophisticated and spiritually advanced, it will lack Christ. But anyone wishing to receive the favour and privileges of the establishment or even lead a normal life in the world with money, material comfort, and such like, will have to make a similar commitment to the 'beast'. They will have to accept its 'mark' in return for being allowed full participation as a citizen of a global government.

This is only an imaginary speculation. Nevertheless, the signs of the times are pointing in this direction for those whose spiritual eyes are in any way open, and who have paid attention to the warnings we have been given from tradition and over the past few years. In the Christian version of the end times this is the outcome of our love affair with the anti-traditional nature and materialism of modern technology.

The Fox's Prophecy

It is not just in the great myths and religions of the world that the end times are foretold. *The Fox's Prophecy* is an English poem written in about 1870 by a Mr. D.W. Nash about whom not much seems to be known though he was clearly someone with a deep love for the English countryside. The scene is set on a beautiful crisp November morning in the Cotswolds when *the diamonds of the hoar-frost were sparkling in the sun* and *the varied tints of autumn still lingered in the wood.* A huntsman, Tom Hill by name who was a real person, becomes separated from his hounds and, turning to look for them, he is suddenly *struck by an aged fox that sat beneath a tree.* Surprise turns to astonishment when the fox fixes his *sparkling eye, which shone with an unearthly fire* on the huntsman and addresses him *like a Christian man.* The talking fox says that as the last of his race he has been given the power of prophecy, and he proceeds to unfold a vision of the future which is not a happy one.

The fox is clearly no ordinary beast but a supernatural being, and the fact that he is the last of his race tells us that the supernatural is on the point of being chased away from the everyday world and to its great detriment because without some contact with the supernatural we fall into complete materialism, as indeed we have. Materialism does not just mean that the spiritual is no longer regarded as real. It means that everything is sacrificed to the utilitarian and the monetary, hence the modern obsession with the economy and the destruction of beauty unless it can be made economically viable.

The fox first predicts the end of hunting, but he says he regrets this because the end of hunting means the end of traditional rural life, of community and living according to the seasons of nature. He says that *not upon these hills alone, the doom of sport shall fall: O'er the broad face of England creeps, The shadow on the wall.* Thus, he equates the demise of foxhunting as going along with a more general decline. It doesn't cause that decline but the state of mind that ends hunting has other much broader effects as well. In a way, and paradoxically to the modern mentality, it shows a disconnect with nature. This is not meant as an argument in favour of foxhunting for sport but simply as a general observation.

The fox continues. *Hedgerow and copse shall cease to shade the ever-widening field* is a prediction that has certainly come true as the English countryside has been decimated by development. But then he says that *The manly sports of England shall vanish one by one; ... The manly blood of England in weaker veins shall run.* England was the first nation to industrialise and reap the benefits of a reduction in infant mortality through such things as improved sanitation and healthcare. In 1800 the infant mortality rate was 33%. In 1870 when the poem was written 26% of children died before their fifth birthday, but now the figure stands at 4%. On the face of it this is an unmitigated good, but nothing is that simple. What is happening in this case is that the weaker are surviving and adverse genetic mutations that would have been weeded out of the stock by natural selection are carrying on and spreading. Forget the moral issues for the moment. On a purely pragmatic level the consequences are what they are, and the fox was right. Moreover, these adverse genetic mutations (and the vast majority of mutations are adverse) do not just have an impact on physical well-being but affect the brain even more as 84% of the genome is active in that organ, more than any other part of the body. This will potentially lead to personality disorders, problems with mental health, and even decline in intelligence. All predicted by the fox in a couple of pithy lines and again further on when he says, *Degenerate sons of manlier sires to lower joys shall fall.*

The fox goes on with his tale of woe as the ancient landmarks sink under the waves of progress, time-honoured creeds go down and traditional faith becomes a joke though there arise a swarm of new religions preached by self-made apostles. Education is dominated by utilitarians who do not teach how to think but what to think. *The only god is gold* needs no comment, and the fox then predicts the consequences of feminism when he says, *The homes where love and peace should dwell, fierce politics shall vex, and unsexed woman strive to prove herself the coarser sex.*

Politicians become coarse demagogues, honour and truth are derided, and *the glory of a thousand years shall end in foul disgrace. Trade shall be held the only good* while the army and navy are cast aside as too expensive to maintain. The wise fox even predicts the mass immigration of recent years. *The footsteps of the invader then England's shore shall know, While home-bred traitors give the hand to England's every foe.* The country becomes *disarmed before the foreigner ... and yields the treasures that she lacked the wisdom to defend.* Who can deny this is exactly what has happened? Are there not many cases of the family silver being sold for short-term profit?

All is not doom and gloom, however. The fox foresees a restoration when *purged by fire and sword, the land her freedom shall regain,* and *taught wisdom by disaster* with *the greed of gold departed ... Old England's sons again shall raise the Altar and the Crown.* At this point the cry of the hounds breaks in on the scene and the fox vanishes leaving the huntsman alone to shake his head in wonder as indeed he might, given that the numinous has just broken in on his everyday world. No one is ever left the same after such an experience.

When I first read this poem I was reminded of the Prophecy of Hermes which is a very different but at the same time similar work from around 300 AD. Contained in the Book of Asclepius, it describes the downfall of ancient Egypt when it abandons the gods. It is different because it is much more religious in tone, but it is similar in that it predicts the tragedy of cultural loss through human ignorance, egotism, and materialism. In the

Egyptian case there is a spiritual restoration when God *cleanses the world from evil, now washing it away with water-floods, now burning it out with fiercest fire, or again expelling it by war and pestilence.* This is proper end times, conclusion of the cycle stuff. The fox's version is simpler and humbler though it too includes a purging by fire.

The fox's view is simpler because it is a peasant's or countryman's version of the end time scenario that is more concerned with national than spiritual loss though there is an overlap. Don't forget the fox may be a supernatural being but he is still a member of the animal kingdom. His prophecy is written not from grand metaphysical insight like the Egyptian one and others, but a deep instinct that comes from being in tune with the environment and a sensitivity to changes which do not arise organically. It lacks the spiritual awareness of more sophisticated versions but makes up for that by its sympathy with the natural and the traditional which serve as guides to right thought and behaviour. The fox realises that the modern world is abandoning these things to go its own way and sees it as being very much the loser by that. He speaks from an awareness of natural rhythms and cycles, and knows that when human beings turn their back on nature and act on egotism they fall into materialism and greed which lead to disaster. But he has no real understanding of the spiritual processes involved behind all that so the restoration he foretells is of a much more elementary nature. His prophecy is accurate as far as it goes but it doesn't go far enough.

Part Three

God and the Soul

Meditation and Its Limitations

Meditation is often presented as a remedy for the problems that accompany living in a body with a self-conscious mind, problems we can associate with the idea of duality, the sense that there is the everyday 'me' and then there is the world, everything outside of our self, and some kind of relationship must be forged between the two. For brief moments they can exist in a state of harmony but more frequently, especially in a fallen world such as ours which has disharmony written into it, there is conflict between them which results in tension and disturbance. In meditation the split between these two contrasting aspects of life can be overcome as they are made, or seem to be made, one. In this way suffering is healed and the one meditating knows peace.

But is that the aim of life in this world? Are we here merely to escape being here, having learnt or gained nothing from the experience of duality? Putting it differently, does duality exist only to be destroyed or, if you prefer, seen as non-existent in reality? Assuming we emerge from a spiritual world of oneness and bliss, why would we leave that world only to re-enter it the same as we left? That makes no sense in a rational universe, and we know the universe is rational because it is based on order and law, and reason exists. If impersonal bliss is the goal and the spiritual end is to lose all sense of self and be absorbed into oneness, there is no point in coming to Earth. No point in reaching for the good, the beautiful, and the true, no point in love because all these things dissolve in pure oneness. Yes, even love which depends for its fulfilment and expression on the reality of the person. Universal compassion is not love and is a pale substitute for it.

Through meditation we may escape the alienation and suffering to be found in the physical world of duality and conflict, but we might also escape the good which becomes an illusion of the unenlightened.

The sensible conclusion is that we come to this world to learn to be more than naked spirit. That would entail having a personal relationship with God and that means to be fully a person. Spiritual approaches that emphasise the impersonal aspect of deity fall short of the truth. There is a part of God that is pure being, but this is a property of his essential 'I' ness as is implied in the English phrase "I am" in which I comes before am. There is no 'am-ness' without a prior I.

Therefore, we should see impersonal being as an aspect of God's overall reality as Person not a higher part of it, which is why one can say that a theistic approach which sees God as personal includes, while the impersonal approach excludes.

What is included or excluded? Everything! It is creation and the reality of created beings. These have no substance in impersonal spirituality. Neither you nor I have any fundamental reality. And if you think about it, how could the personal arise from the impersonal? The theory of those who hold to this notion is that it comes about through faulty identification, as pure consciousness mistakes itself for the form it takes. But why should consciousness do this if there was no self to do it to begin with?

Many of those who pursue the path of impersonal spirituality believe they must overcome the sense of themselves as individual beings, but the impression of a universal oversoul reached in deep meditation is just a doorway. One needs to go through this door and on through the outer courts of the temple to the sanctum sanctorum where is revealed the personal nature of God. The impersonal state of bliss known in meditation is like the formless chaos of the void on which cosmic order must be imposed to bring it into the clear light of day and give it cohesion and coherence. God is not formless being which is simply the wax on which he imprints form. God is a Person who creates in order to have relationships with other persons. Going back to the idea of exclusion, the impersonal oneness sought by some in meditation might be seen as a form of separation in that it sunders spirit from matter. The One becomes all and the Many nothing, jettisoned as a stain on the pristine whiteness of pure being. But a better understanding shows that we come to Earth to learn to bring together the two poles of life, oneness and individuality, in our person, and to make thereby a cosmic marriage not a divorce.

These comments are not meant to dismiss meditation but to put it in perspective. One of the consequences of the flattening out tendencies of the end times is greater breadth, less depth. This means that spiritual teachings and tools, hitherto the preserve of an elite or intended for a select group of properly qualified individuals, become available on a mass level, but their wise and judicious use does not automatically follow, especially if promoted by instructors lacking spiritual insight or else detached from their appropriate metaphysical background and used for palliative healing.

There are many benefits to be gained from meditation in terms of inner peace and a sense of communion with what we might conceive of as universal spirit, but the practice can also desensitise you to other people, and their joys and sufferings purely as human beings. You can become too detached, too wrapped up in your inner self and your higher consciousness, cut off from the outer world and even from God. Because that's what meditation can do. Who needs God as the personal living God if you believe you are God in his most spiritualised aspect? Who needs other people if you are absorbed in self-centred bliss?

Some of those drawn to meditation are like spiritual sunbathers who want to experience God as a formless being in which they can become blissfully immersed. They do want love, but it is a passive kind of love they seek, a diffused glow instead of a focused and concentrated beam of light. It is a generalised love, quite different to that of the Christian who aspires to love and be loved by God as a person. And really if love is not personal, it is not love at all but something else which may partake of love's warmth but lacks its fire. An abstract love like this is not what Jesus spoke of in his two great commandments, and if you do not first love God, the living God, then love for your neighbour is just an external thing, more academic than real which is something we do very often see in spiritual groups.

Meditation can attune the meditator to the soul, but, if not seen as subsidiary to proper awareness of God, it can also be a spiritual diversion, especially in the end times when a certain sensitive type may try to withdraw from the challenges, travails, and general chaos of the outer world into an inner sanctum of peace in which he seeks to disappear. The *via negativa* is an effective path to follow to break the spiritual aspirant's identification with the world but once its lessons have been learned he must move on to include the *via positiva*.

Consciousness and Christ

According to standard esoteric teachings, human souls come to this Earth to evolve their consciousness, this being the perfect environment in which to do that given the sense of separation to be found here. It's somewhat like a child being turfed out of the secure family home where everything is done for it to make its own way in the world and as a result become a mature, responsible adult, able to engage with life creatively and thereby contribute to the world in a positive manner. These teachings assume reincarnation and say we come back here many times, seeking experience and means of expression to grow as souls. This is linked to the doctrine of reaping what you sow with the consequence that everything we do, and possibly even think, sets up a flow of psychic energy which we must deal with. It may manifest materially as external circumstances and conditions or internally as character traits, but we are responsible for all that we are. This is not to punish but to teach. We evolve in this way until we are able to raise our consciousness to the spiritual level while in an earthly body. It's more complicated than that but this is the theory in a nutshell version.

Sometimes these teachings picture us as like cells in the body of a greater being which would be the spirit that stands behind our sun. This being or Solar Logos is also evolving and would be part of a Galactic Being who, in turn, would form part of the being who stands behind the whole universe who would, in this scheme of things, be God. There is a pleasing symmetrical order to this scenario, and it makes sense on an intellectual level. I believe it to have a great deal of truth in it with the solar and stellar spirits as something like archangels, and so on upwards.

There is a problem with this vision though. It doesn't fit in with Christian teaching. Esotericists realise this and, as a result, tend to discard Christianity, reducing Christ to a great spiritual teacher or Head of a Spiritual Hierarchy that oversees humanity, or else picture him as the Solar Logos and say this was what was meant by Son of God. You can absorb most other spiritual approaches into this one which is what its partisans generally do, but you cannot really absorb Christ. Not without making him something other than what he said he was or altering his teachings to mean something other than what he says they mean. Christ didn't talk about evolving consciousness and he was not inclusive. He said that he was the Way, the Truth, and the Life. That is unequivocal. He is not part of some all-purpose spirituality, but goes beyond mere spirituality to something higher, deeper and truer, something approaching proper holiness. Christ taught that we should love God whom we could see revealed in him. This is extreme to say the least, but it is what he taught, and if we believe in Christ, we must believe that.

Is it possible to reconcile these two teachings? Many people don't bother. They believe one or the other, but I find myself in the tricky position of thinking there is truth in both. I do believe that human souls are supposed to be evolving their consciousness, and this Earth serves as the background for that, a kind of playpen in which we can build things though what we are really building is ourselves. But I also believe that Christ goes beyond that. This means that spirituality and evolving consciousness is one thing, but Christ is another. He comes to the worldly and the spiritual alike and offers them both something more. The spiritual may be further along the path to God as things stand but the wonder of Christ is that anyone can come to him from any background and is accepted by him if they give themselves heart and soul to him, and this acceptance will transform their soul to a higher degree than any self-pursued spirituality can ever do. You may be building a humble village church or a grand cathedral, but both are hollow structures without the light of Christ illumining them from within.

Could it be that before the advent of Christ scenario 1 operated? Human souls reincarnated after a period in the spiritual realms to further their spiritual evolution and this proceeded in a certain direction, developing all aspects of the whole being, unless brought to a close by the attainment of Buddhist Nirvana meaning a complete disidentification with the phenomenal world and, in a sense, rejection of creation. But Christ came to bring a higher understanding, one in which the soul could be made like him by allowing him into itself. Any soul on any evolutionary level could do this though naturally the more developed the soul, the more of Christ it could absorb and express. Thus, the path of spiritual evolution exists and so does the path of Christ, but this latter brings more of divine reality to the picture. For instance, an evolving soul might, in esoteric parlance, have opened all its psychic energy centres including that at the crown of the head, but unless it has fully accepted Christ it is still operating in the spiritual world rather than the true Heaven of Christ which is a new creation containing more of divine being than can ever be attained just through evolution.

Much more remains to be done if one is to develop a proper understanding of how Christ impacts and goes beyond standard issue spirituality, but this is a start inasmuch as it draws a clear distinction between Christ and everything else.

These two scenarios have relevance to our theme of the end times. These exist in pagan thought as the last and most decadent phase of a grand cosmic cycle, most notably in Hinduism where the symptoms of decline are laid out clearly in the Puranas. It is not known when these were written but scholars seem to agree that it would have been between 250 and 900 AD or thereabouts, though they would certainly have existed in oral form before that. Nonetheless, the possibility remains that there is some Christian influence, particularly regarding the avatar of the god Vishnu who comes to restore truth and justice at the end of the age. This is Kalki but it seems he may originally have been called *Karki* which means white, possibly after the horse he rides, and one might speculate that this is none other than Christ in an Indian form. For although Christ was born in a particular time and place, he came for the whole world and his spiritual, and even salvific, influence extends to all religions that allow themselves to be open to him, the bhakti movement in India and the figure of the Bodhisattva in Buddhism being obvious examples. This influence operates primarily on the spiritual level and does not depend on cultural contact in the physical world though that may sometimes be present too.

The spiritual path has always existed in some form but before Christ it required heroic efforts to break free of the chains of matter; witness the extraordinary feats of ascetism performed by the early Indian sages. The Buddha himself tried this path which shows it was a time-honoured spiritual discipline in his day. The Buddha may have abandoned it in its extreme form, but asceticism continued to be an essential element of spiritual practice because the material and the spiritual opposed each other until Christ. What Christ did through his death and resurrection was redeem fallen matter so that henceforth matter could be the vessel for spirit and was no longer its enemy. This still requires the submission of the material to the spiritual for which a degree of ascetic purification remains necessary, but it also means that anyone who allows Christ to be born and grow within them, which is what faith really means, is saved from the grip of matter and the cycle of births and deaths in *samsaric* realms, meaning the many worlds outside of the true Heaven where Christ is king and the perfection of love is accomplished. Now, in the end times, it becomes increasingly important for the aspirant to align his spirit with that of Christ because deception abounds, not least in the spiritual sphere, and the knowledge of Christ is the only thing that can save one from that.

The Root of Reality

What is the foundational spiritual quality? The one that lies behind every other manifested or unmanifested quality or state or even that which gives rise to qualities and states. I suggest it is freedom. Others might point to being or love, but freedom must exist first for love to be. Some metaphysicians speak of a state beyond being which they call non-being. This is the primordial state of freedom.

If freedom is fundamental to spirit, then that which opposes freedom is anti-spiritual. However, there is anti-spiritual and there is non-spiritual. Matter is non-spiritual because it is the complementary pole to spirit in the manifested state, but it is not anti-spiritual when properly ordered. It only becomes so when in a fallen condition. If it, as it were, forgets its prime function and seeks to serve itself rather than spirit it then becomes anti-spiritual. For consciousness to be bound to matter represents a loss of freedom and, although this occurs to advance a potentially greater freedom in that there should be a reaction to the constriction and a conscious attempt to rise above it, the risk is that consciousness may succumb to its material entrapment and lose freedom. The reason that evil exists is because of freedom but it is also the reason that life seeks expression and growth. If the question is "Why?", the answer is "Freedom."

We live at a time when freedom is being increasingly curtailed though this is not always as obvious as it might be. In one sense, there is more freedom for the human being now than ever. The unfolding patterns of evolution and the growth of consciousness have brought this about. The focus on the self inevitably causes the demand for freedom since freedom is what lies at the root of our self as its base principle just as it does for God. We are created in his image. But there are counter currents which seek to restrict this freedom. The communism of the 20th century was one such crude but effective attempt. However, it failed because it was coercive. The devil seeks to corrupt human souls but for spiritual corruption to be properly successful it must be willingly chosen. This is because of free will which God will not contravene, and the devil cannot.

A question that has always troubled thoughtful religious people is how can what God creates go against God? If God is both omnipotent and good how does evil arise? This raises a dilemma that cannot be ignored by any spiritually concerned person.

There is no conflict on the spiritual level between God being the author of everything and human beings having complete free will. There is no logical reason why God cannot create lots of potential little gods out of himself which then, to become actual gods, have to develop themselves which they do through their experiences in the various worlds of being and becoming, worlds of choice, of duality, of testing and of self-expression. Christians say God creates out of nothing, and as he is God, he can do that. That's what being God means. He is both a spiritual being and spiritual being itself, the personal Creator but also unmanifest reality. However, one might put this in a slightly different way and say that God creates out of himself. So, we are created out of God and in his image which means with free will. The possibility of evil arises because without it we would not be able voluntarily to turn to the good. That still does not answer why beings should turn to evil or why they should oppose God and creation, but if free will really is free then this is always a possibility. The created want to be the creator. The fact of a free self might make some look for freedom outside God instead of within him, though that just means they have become the slaves of their own egos and lost real freedom. The doctrine of the Fall helps explain why evil arose in human terms, and why both this world and human nature were corrupted to the extent that the Incarnation was needed to help put them right. The ultimate mystery of evil may not be solved by this. It is simply pushed back into the spiritual world where first it appeared, but to take the first step in addressing that mystery we can say that evil is the unfortunate by-product of freedom.

For those who question why God does not directly create the perfect gods he wants us to become without taking the risk that we might go bad, the answer clearly is that if he did that then we wouldn't be gods in our own right. We would merely be clones of him. We must make ourselves gods from the raw material he gives us. It might be objected that if this raw material comes from him, it should be him and so should not have the capacity for evil or to go wrong, but that is to misunderstand the nature of free will. If it really is free, then it will have the capacity to go wrong. The idea of evil is built into the possibility of knowing the good. It all comes back to freedom.

With the coming of the end times the question of freedom becomes a pressing concern. The evolving state of human consciousness has led to demands for more freedom, but this is often on the level of the ego and its desires, consequently it is an anti-spiritual freedom that is demanded, one rooted in the material. True freedom lies in willingly making the right choices, and that is the need of the moment. At the same time, there are forces on both the physical and nonphysical planes that seek to restrict freedom for physical and nonphysical ends. This is what we must be alive to in these times.

In centuries past human beings could be controlled relatively easily. A more evolved consciousness, such as exists in our day in the sense of greater self-awareness, requires a subtler level of control. But still, it must be said, it is not very subtle. The reality behind the events of 2020 should have been obvious but it wasn't to the majority, and even now when evidence is emerging that the response to the problem was way over the top, most people still won't accept it. I suppose no one likes to think they have been played for a fool.

Then there is the matter of the weather. The fact that it is not and never has been fixed is being used as an excuse to bring in ever greater controls which we are told we must accept for our own good and that of others, an always effective ploy to persuade people to submit to regulation. Cost of living increases serve the same purpose as does the move to replace cash with digital currency. All these things point in the same direction. Loss of freedom.

And there is more. Almost everyone nowadays uses computers in some form throughout the greater part of their waking existence. Computers are based on a technology in which measurement, control, and quantification are fundamental. Control and regulation. There is no real freedom in a computer, and our use of them affects our consciousness and the way we think. I have already made the point that technology is not neutral as it frames the way we view life. Our minds adapt to the technology we use. The use of computers makes us think and even perceive more like computers. This leads to a reduction of spiritual freedom, never mind that our dependence on computers also reduces our own inner sensibility as external substitutes become more realistic.

The greatest achievement of the rapidly fading Western civilisation was the development of human freedom. This had its negative side when it tipped over into self-indulgence, decadence, and all the rest that we know so well. Even freedom, the greatest good, must be balanced and directed into proper channels which truth is expressed so well in the saying from the Book of Common Prayer that *"in his service is perfect freedom."* The highest freedom is to be found in Christ because that is the flowering of spiritual freedom, but this too must grow from the soil of individual freedom. Without that there can be no eventual spiritual freedom.

The end times demand that we remain alert to the constraints on freedom in every area of life. The grand purpose of freedom is to enable us to know God, but if our freedom is not directed to that end, it will turn bad so our task now is twofold. First, to resist the loss of freedom and, second, to use our freedom wisely which means to open it up to God. For only in God is true and lasting freedom to be found.

The Omnipotence of God

Is God all powerful or not? If he is, why does he not intervene in human affairs more or even at all? If he is not, can he really be considered a proper God? There are arguments on both sides, but there is also a standpoint from which both are true, and which can reconcile apparent contradictions.

Let's start with the basic argument in favour of a supreme Creator, the One without a second from whom all things derive. This is an intellectual argument which is fine though it is not the point from which I would personally start. That would be intuitive or from the point of direct knowing. This, however, cannot be shared and could be seen as open to error through wishful thinking or some other kind of mental/emotional distortion. When all is said and done, we take the subjective route in matters of belief but in sharing our beliefs an objective stance, as in one deriving from reason and logic, is usually more persuasive. So, here is one of the classic arguments in favour of God.

Everything that exists has a cause but there must ultimately be something that is the cause of everything else, a causeless cause, or the process could not get started. Something must kick everything else off and be the ground from which everything else grows. No uncaused first cause means no nothing. Literally. There cannot be anything but there cannot be nothing either as nothing implies an absence, but there can't be absence unless there is presence to begin with. What would there be if there wasn't anything? Don't go there!

This something cannot be reliant on anything else or it would be an effect and therefore not the first cause. It must be self-sufficient. It cannot be limited because there is nothing that could limit it, everything else deriving from it itself and subordinate to it. Not being limitable means it is all-powerful.

It is (is, not has) Being-Consciousness or timeless Awareness, existing in total autonomy on a formless level, form being something that comes about along with time and space as the structure for creation. It must be Being-Consciousness because otherwise there could be neither being nor consciousness deriving from it.

Properly trained theologians could develop this train of thought more thoroughly and they have done so. The point I wish to make here though is that this line of thought affirms the omnipotence of God, given that he is the cause, ground, root, source, and fountainhead of everything else. He is the Creator, and this universe is his creation. He can change any part of it at any moment by a thought. Or, at least, he could do that if he had not renounced some of his power. And this is precisely what he has done.

In creating individual creatures with free will God has given up power. He must do this or we could not have free will. If he could intervene as and when he felt like it our free will would be a mockery, something that could go so far but no further. Conditional free will is not properly free. It is true that the rules of the universe which God has set up do not allow for unlimited expression of free will. If it is exercised against creation there will be consequences, call it karma, reaping what you sow, or whatever. But that is a different thing. There may be consequences of free will exercised in the wrong way, but our freedom in itself is still sacrosanct, never overridden.

God gives part of his creation, maybe all his creation eventually, free will for two reasons. The first is love. For love really to be it must be free. Constrained love, necessary love, automatic love? It makes no sense. Only creatures with free will can love, and only they can be loved in the highest, most rewarding sense.

The second reason is that this makes creation more interesting for God. If his creatures start creating themselves, it will make creation come alive for God in ways that would not have been possible if he alone acted. Think of a universe endlessly expanding from within, one that is dynamic, free, without regular or predictable pattern, with a bit of grit in it that makes pearls. That is much more exciting than a clockwork universe. Human free will is like the little lack of balance that can take creation in intriguing and unpredictable new directions. You might think that nothing is unpredictable to God but even if he sees everything at one time, it is still new to him as he sees it. If it doesn't come directly from him then even if he sees it before it happens from our limited perspective, it is still new to him.

Human freedom can be bad as well as good. Giving us free will is a risk. If we exercise this will in accordance with the laws of God and creation, then the sky's the limit, but if we go against those laws then we become creatively destructive. It's not hard to see what the tendency is at the moment, and it may be that there is a fail-safe device installed in creation that will not let the process go too far. Myth and religious tradition tell us that is exactly what has happened in the past. But for God the potential gain is worth the risk because a universe without freedom would be a semi-dead universe.

Here then is my conclusion. God, or the creative Mind behind everything, is omnipotent but he renounces some of his power to give it to us in the form of free will, and that means he is no longer omnipotent.

Now, this leads on to an important point. In the past human beings have accepted the omnipotence of God and this has often led to varying degrees of fatalism. We just must accept God's will. But what if God wants partners rather than servants? Partners who can work with him in making creation more magnificent instead of workers whose only function is to maintain it. This means that we must accept our power and use it wisely. As potential co-creators we are called to work with God but not for him. Certainly, we work according to the laws of creation and under the overall headship of God, with life rather than against it, so our work is loving cooperation as opposed to individualism. A core spiritual teaching is to be individual but not individualistic. But God gave us power so that we could exercise it and work alongside him. This is where we are now and where the changes in consciousness that have come about over the last few centuries should be taking us. At the moment, our heightened sense of individuality has brought more evil than good as it is working out on the material plane, but as we evolve it may be that it will begin to transfer itself, in some of us anyway, to the spiritual plane and then God's transference of power to mankind will start to bear good fruit.

To see how this idea of partnership with God works let us take the example of prayer. Many people would say why bother praying since God must know what we want or need. No doubt he does, but perhaps our praying for something opens the door to potentially receiving it. It makes us active participants in a process instead of passive bystanders, and in this way we become co-workers with God. This can be compared to a law of spiritual teaching which states that in order to receive an answer the student must ask a question. This shows his ripeness to receive but also makes him an active participant who, in a certain manner, determines the answer himself rather than a piece of wax waiting to be stamped with whatever image the one stamping chooses.

One of the positive aspects of the present day, and, yes, there are some, is that those who are drawn to the spiritual path are more likely to try to understand and not just accept which means they can engage more deeply with reality and start to prepare themselves to become at some future time genuine co-workers with God who can contribute to the enlargement and greater flourishing of the universe in a way that those who unquestioningly accept are not able to do.

What Is the Soul?

This is the most important question of the day but for most people it doesn't even arise. Either they think there is no such thing as a soul, a spiritual element to their being, or else they believe their soul is who and what they feel themselves to be here and now. Something no different to their everyday personality. I would say even most religious people don't know what the soul is, especially those who don't believe it exists before birth in this world, so let me attempt a definition. The question is important because if we know what we really are then we would know what we should be doing and where we should be going. If we don't know what we are how can we determine the correct way to think or act or where to direct our aspiration?

The soul is the core of our being. It is that aspect of the self that is joined to the eternal and which takes us beyond the mundane and the material, and imparts the sense of the sacred. It is the source of our individuality and our freedom. Without the soul these essential elements of what it is to be human would not exist. They do not derive from matter, which is why a materialistic approach to life has no explanation for them and must, if it is to be logically consistent with itself, deny they exist.

The soul is a spiritual being which is to say its location and natural focus is the spiritual realm which is the plane of consciousness. In a sense, the soul is pure subjectivity but it needs the experience of objectivity, otherwise known as duality, to bring it out of itself and enable it to grow. This means to become first aware of and then able to engage with the wider reality of God's creation and eventually God himself. The soul in its own world is naturally one with God but passively so. To know God in a deeper way and consciously share in his being, it must externalise itself which it does in the material world where there is I and That. The challenges it faces in such an environment give it the opportunity to grow.

This is a process with risk attached. When the soul leaves its spiritually secure state it is neither good nor evil. The tendency to one or the other condition is brought out by its reaction to the dualistic world. It can consciously align itself with the greater reality of God or it can reject this reality and become fixated on itself. This goes deeper than simple belief. I call it the orientation of the heart. It is a matter of feeling. Not emotion which is based on personal reaction to stimuli but innate response to spiritual reality, a kind of answering resonance of the self to God. This should make clear that true religion is not following a set of rules or teachings but the positive opening of the heart to the higher spiritual power, higher because there are many forces in the universe, but we are talking about the Creator not anything in creation.

My teachers, who spoke from the spiritual plane as related in the book *Meeting the Masters*, told me that **the greater part of you remains with us**. This implies that only an aspect of the soul takes earthly incarnation. The soul is more than the earthly personality, which is its representative in three-dimensional existence, but the two are intimately linked forming a whole. What one does impacts the other even if only a fraction of the totality of what the soul is manifests in our ordinary existence.

It is the soul that evolves which means unfolds its spiritual potential, but it does so by means of the earthly personality and what it experiences and expresses in this world. There is a symbiotic relationship between the two, and although ultimately only the soul remains, it is coloured by the personality which eventually dissolves into it as sugar does into tea, thereby imparting its flavour. The wise do not identify themselves with their personality but they do not reject it either. It is part of the totality of their being even if it is certainly not the central core. That remains the soul.

There are spiritual states even beyond the soul, though to differentiate between the two I would designate these higher states as divine. We are called to conjoin our soul with these higher states in divine union but even when that takes place our individuality remains what it is. Expanded, deepened, divinised, but still the soul.

The distinction between the soul and the earthly personality is sometimes expressed by referring to them as the higher and lower selves which carries the sense that the soul is our real self with the earthly self merely its representative in the material world. This latter is an expression of the soul but cut down to fit into the much more limited earthly conditions (hence the feeling of spiritual claustrophobia sensitive people may experience) and tailored to the lessons it is due to learn as well as the tasks it is scheduled to accomplish. It is also that which causes the rise of the ego which occurs when the earthly self assumes dominance over the spiritual. We all have this ego. Don't assume only conventionally egotistical people have it. It takes different forms but is present in every human being. It is the real original sin.

Nothing said here supports the belief that the soul is a spiritual being which has become trapped in matter, whether for reasons of karma, wrong thinking, some kind of spiritual trauma, or whatever, and that the material world is therefore something to escape from. That's the Gnostic view (see earlier chapter) and it is mistaken. It has many modern equivalents which are all variations on the theme that somehow the soul is good and the lower self bad. That is not the case. The soul incarnates in matter, which is created by God and therefore good even if it has become corrupted, in order to further its evolution as in unfoldment of its potential. It avails itself of the possibilities of the material world to develop itself. Through separation it becomes more conscious of itself and better able to make positive choices consciously thus eventually fitting itself to become a god in its own right.

Our material self is not evil, illusionary, or in any way wrong except when it becomes an end in itself. It is certainly limiting but that is the point of it. Think of it as a constriction which focuses the attention of consciousness on an environment in which God is not obviously present. That gives it the opportunity to develop itself and the greater self from which it derives in a way that would not be possible on more spiritual levels in which conflict and challenge are not present. Through the lower self we become aware of a problem and are given the wherewithal to solve it. Or not as the case may be. For this is also a test. How does the self react to God when he is seemingly not there? This is an examination of the heart. A correctly oriented heart turns to God in some way. One of ill will, and let's remind ourselves that faith is a matter of will not intellect, does not.

The Gnostic view is half right and half wrong. We do have a spiritual self which exists in a higher plane of being, but it does not become trapped in matter because of some sin or nefarious activity of evil spirits. It descends to learn, descending meaning accepting a more circumscribed state of existence. Matter is not evil although the material world is not the spiritual which means it is subject to the law of entropy. But it has a function and our appearance in it has a purpose.

Speaking of Gnosticism, I should mention the other main fallacy of that approach to spirituality. The clue is in the name. Salvation for the Gnostics comes through knowledge but no amount of spiritual knowledge will get the earthly human to heaven. Salvation comes through grace not knowledge, and grace is bestowed on those who make themselves worthy of it through love. Love means primarily love of God and that comes when the soul turns to its Creator, opening up its heart and mind. This is our problem. Our hearts and mind are closed, and they are so because we are fixated on the material self.

But the Gnostics were also right. The pre-eminence of love, spiritual love not the earthly variety with which it is often confused by sentimentalists, is no justification for ignorance. Knowledge is also important. In fact, the more one loves God or Truth, the more one wants to understand and to know. We have a heart and mind and there are spiritual correspondences to these two. Both must be satisfied. If spiritual love is missing today so too is spiritual knowledge, which is why mainstream religion is so unsatisfactory for many people. Spiritual knowledge is not just facts and figures, intellectual knowledge. It is that but it is more, for it derives primarily from the intuition. Nowadays there exists an abundance of writings about the spiritual worlds, an Alexandrian library's worth, but all this is flat and without life until animated by an individual's own intuition.

Love and wisdom. These are the two attributes of the developed soul. Both must be pursued by the aspiring disciple until he gets to the point where he sees they are facets of the same thing.

The main problems facing the incarnate personality in the end times are related, though might seem opposites. They are no knowledge of the soul and false knowledge of the soul. These problems have always existed, but the nature of these times is that they become more serious. They are also more significant because this is a time when decisions have deep consequences, and the choices you make bring you closer to or take you further away from God. The intensification of the material side of manifestation obscures the spiritual which means that either the spiritual is denied, as in materialism, or, if it is in any way seen, it is through the distorting lens of the material which has marked with its imprint both the mind and the sense of self. Thus, either the soul is not seen, or it is seen through heavy contamination and misconstrued.

The solution is humility and detachment, and a concerted effort to lift the mind up away from where earthly influences operate. And one way to do this is to meditate on the colours blue and gold. More specifically, azure blue and gold. Visualisation on these colours will purify the mind and attune it to the world of the soul where lower influences cannot enter. Blue and gold are the colours of the heavens, not just the physical heaven of sun and sky but the spiritual too which is primary, and they oppose and counteract the red and black qualities of the Kali Yuga. This exercise may seem simple and, as with any such exercise, its effectiveness depends on proper motivation, but by building these colours into your consciousness, you can start to lift it up out of earthly darkness into realms of clarity and light. Not coincidentally, the ceiling of an Egyptian Pharoah's tomb was decorated with golden stars on a deep blue background, showing him the way to heaven.

The Expansion of Consciousness

Some people believe the highest spiritual state is one in which the sense of separation between the soul and God has been so obliterated that the soul has, in effect, become God. There remains no individual self at all. This is the basic theme of Buddhism and certain forms of Hinduism. As it is of the modern Western derivation of ancient Eastern mysticism which is Oneness spirituality, though that is a second-tier simplification of its inspiring models. There are Christian versions of this too which are probably influenced by Zen with a dash of Meister Eckhart and a pinch of Plotinus. In these beliefs, and they are beliefs notwithstanding the fact that there is some kind of experience in which self seems to be dissolved, self is the cause of sin and what must be eradicated is not just the possibility of sin but that which made that possibility possible. This can appear the apex of mysticism, the version that stands above and subsumes all the different religions, but it is better defined as a particular mystical experience which may point to an aspect of the soul's relationship with God but does not cover it in its totality nor indicate its ideal end.

What we have here is killing the patient to save him even if the intended result is not death but a form of eternal life. It is not, though, the highest form. Self may be the cause of everything bad, but it is also the cause of the good, including goodness itself. And it is what lies behind love. God created for a reason, that being the joy of relationship. The advocates of no self deny the purpose of creation. They would return to the non-manifest state of darkness or limitless light. It makes no difference how you envision it as it is the boiling down of everything to no-thing. It may be possible to return consciousness to the pool of infinity whence it arose but that is not what God wants nor what Christ offered when he came to redeem the world from its spiritual darkness. Christ came to heal the soul, not to show us a way to kill it. God and creation together is more than just God by himself, and no self means no love, no beauty, no goodness, no expression or growth through time. Nothing but resting in eternal peace. That is fine if you have a limited view of spiritual life but there is much more, and to know this more one should seek to transform the self not to eradicate it. The advocates of no self are turning their back on God in his creative, expressive, and personal mode, and retreating to a passive form of consciousness which resembles the spiritual womb. But God wants us to be born and to be alive and to partake in his creative glory. He wants us to know day as well as night, and then add to the beauty of creation ourselves. This we cannot do if we have no self. Then we add precisely nothing. In the words of William Blake, *"God appears and God is Light to those poor souls who dwell in Night, but does a Human Form display to those that dwell in Realms of Day."* The personal is more than the impersonal.

If the spiritual path does not demand the absolute negation of self, what then does it entail? It is obvious that it is the self, in one form or another, that is at the root of the spiritual problem, and if it is not to be snuffed out nor can it be left as it is. Its transformation is what lies at the heart of the spiritual project, and that does indeed require an aspect of it to die, the aspect, in fact, with which we are most identified. This is the reality of no self, but it is attachment to the phenomenal self that must die so the spiritual can be born or, if not born since the phenomenal self can only be in the first place because the spiritual self already is, then grow to mature and full expression.

The expansion of consciousness is a phrase that has long been current in esoteric and mystical circles. I've used it myself in the past because one normally expresses oneself in the language of the day, but also because I wasn't thinking too deeply about what it implies.

What, then, does it imply? To begin with, is expansion of consciousness necessarily a spiritual thing? One may assume so based on an evolutionary understanding of human unfoldment and the idea that the universe exists as a vehicle for the growth of consciousness. In that sense, it is spiritual. Human beings can grow out of their limited earthbound type of consciousness into higher states of multidimensional being. But they can do this through drugs, and there is nothing spiritual about drugs or the states they bestow. Drugs can give the impression of love, bliss, oneness, and all that, as can some forms of mental illness, but this is not spiritual because it relates to effects not inner transformation. Meditation and other spiritual techniques can also bring about heightened states of consciousness, but the subject is not fundamentally changed by that. He may think he is, and he may act in a particular way as a result, but inside he is not really changed for one may have many expansions of consciousness and still remain the same fallen, unredeemed human ego at core. This is true even if the expansionary experiences do not just extend the circumference of the circle of consciousness but take the circle to a sphere. In these cases, the subject may act as though ego has been transcended but he is the same person, responding to his experience by imitating what he thinks is the type of being that would be stabilised in this experience. For note that these expansions of consciousness are all just temporary anyway.

That is why all proper spiritual teachers tell meditators not to imagine they can do without prayer. The old dream of fallen human nature is to think we can reach godhood without God. This is a lie designed to appeal to the spiritually avaricious ego. It's what tempted Eve to bite the apple and it's what tempts many would-be mystics today. Real spirituality without God is not possible.

On a simple linguistic level we can say that something that expands still has the same centre which leads us to point out that from the spiritual perspective it is the transformation of the centre that is the issue not its expansion. This is not to say that souls in heaven do not have a transfigured state of being. Of course they do, but that is because they have taken on the mind of Christ and no spiritual practice can enable that. It is dependent on the soul giving itself to God through Christ and then becoming the recipient of grace. It may be argued that this is just a different way of expressing the same thing, expanding consciousness and taking on the mind of Christ is six of one and half a dozen of the other, but the way you express yourself matters because it both reflects and forms the way you think. If you think of the spiritual journey in terms of expanding consciousness you are thinking of it in terms of what the ego can gain and how it can grow. To reach a truly transfigured consciousness is only possible through taking on the mind of Christ by the sacrifice of self, and that can only happen when the soul loves Christ asking nothing for itself. Everything else is just to make the soul grow by applying some kind of external stimulus. This alone grows the soul from within which is the only true way.

These two concepts, eradicating self and expanding consciousness, represent two different approaches to spiritual reality, and, as opposites often do, they have a certain similarity to each other for they both concern mistaken ideas about the self. The former would melt it down like a candle so that nothing remains with the idea that the life in it would then be poured into the pool of universal life. The latter would blow it up like a balloon so that it takes in more and more of universal life though its intrinsic selfhood remains at the centre. You might call these the mystical and magical paths, and they each have different elements of the truth but neither has the whole. It is in Christ alone that the whole truth is revealed. He showed that the path leads from the Transfiguration to the Crucifixion to the Resurrection and Ascension. On this journey the self is not killed. It is transformed into something new though this does require that it die to itself. The mystics are right that the self, as we know it, must go, but wrong because it is only the self as we know it that dies at the Crucifixion. The magicians are right that the self can become a god, but it is not the phenomenal self that can do this for that is the barrier to godhood. The key is to distinguish between the earthly self, the one we are currently conscious of that is the creation of our own mind caused by identification with our emotions and thoughts, and the real spiritual self. This is the soul which can, when its consciousness has disengaged from the phenomenal world having fully absorbed its lessons, open up to receive and be infused with the divine life of God. Then the self may indeed be said to expand but it is from a new centre which nevertheless was always the real centre that stood behind the false one located in the personal self.

Nothing is thrown away or wasted on the spiritual journey, but the centre of consciousness must be transferred to higher states of being as shown in the great events in the life of Jesus. In this process, the self must die on one level before it can be established on another, though this is a matter of sacrifice not destruction nor expansion.

As the end times progress things are brought into focus or, in the words of C.S. Lewis, they come to a point. *"Have you ever noticed," said Dimble, "that the universe, and every bit of the universe is always hardening and narrowing and coming to a point?"* This is from Lewis' novel *That Hideous Strength*. He continues that as time moves on, *"there is even less room for indecision and choices are even more momentous. Good is always getting better and bad is always getting worse: the possibilities of even apparent neutrality are always diminishing."* The ultimate point to which things are brought is whether they are for or against Christ. This may not necessarily be expressed in terms of conventional Christianity, but it amounts to the alignment or not of the soul with Christ. Spiritual errors which may have been acceptable in the past become less so as they are more revealing of structural flaws in the inner man, particularly in the will. These are the times we are approaching.

The Human Form

We can speculate that our original spiritual form may have been one of light. If it had a shape, it might have been something like a sphere, or that's the closest we can imagine with our three-dimensionally based minds. This is the only way we can conceive of the appearance of the soul, a spiritual being, on its own plane of existence. But when we come to Earth, we acquire the human form we know with eyes, ears, a head, hair, limbs, and so on, all of which are to perform material functions or developed in response to a physical environment. Eyes, ears, and nose are to enable sensory response, their shape and structure determined by that requirement. Hands, fingers, legs, and feet are to allow us to interact with and manipulate the environment. None of these has a spiritual purpose as such, and so my question is, what is the form of souls in heaven? Do they revert to spheres of light with a luminescence determined by the degree of spiritual unfoldment, or do they retain an earthly appearance?

Beauty is one of the attributes of God. A major reason for creation is to allow for the expression of beauty, and, as we currently know it, beauty reaches its apogee in the human being. It makes no sense that this beauty be discarded simply because the functions on which it was initially based are no longer necessary. Therefore, I suggest that one of the reasons for our incarnation as spiritual beings in a material world is to acquire the imprint of the human form which we can take back to our soul selves in the higher worlds to beautify these. This would mean that our souls would still be spheres of light (again conceived in three-dimensional terms), though now greatly expanded and more radiant than they were before if we have succeeded in our spiritual tasks, but they can be expressed in human form. In this physical world we have an outer form and an inner corporeal composition, blood, guts, bodily organs, and the like. In the spiritual world we may have something similar except that the inner body is now the soul, the being of light. This, I submit, is why we all feel a degree of disgust for the inner physical body but not its outer form. We know that our true inner self is the soul.

When visionaries see higher beings, whether it be Jesus or Mary for Christians, or some of the saints, other traditions record similar phenomena, they see a figure. A figure glowing with light but still an individual human figure and one of great beauty. It is sometimes claimed that it is the visionary's own mind that creates the form or else that the spiritual being manifests in this way to appear more familiar. This may be true, but it does not mean that the form is not real as well. We tend to think abstract spirituality is more advanced than a concrete representational sort, but why should both not be included in the perfected end product? After all, God looked at creation and saw that it was good. I think it is a grave error to reduce the spiritual to the formless. There is the inner and the outer, and both together make the whole. The perfection of life is in the perfection of spirit, soul, and body, not just one as in spirit but all three, though naturally with spirit in the hierarchically superior position. But if God is a Trinity, then so are we and all parts of the trinity require completion. The outer form may have been constructed in the physical world and formed according to physical needs, but it is made beautiful by the developing soul and then remains as a spiritually perfected union of the two in the higher worlds.

This line of thought leads us to a consideration of men and women, and the difference between them as well as the purpose for there being two sexes. Science can point to the biological reasons for this, but it is more interesting to speculate on the spiritual reasons, and the clue is in the book of Genesis where it says that God created Eve as a companion for Adam who was lonely. That sounds rather charming, but go behind this simple attempt to explain a deep mystery and you will see that the answer is love.

For life to be expressed it must be expressed dualistically. There must be this and that, or there could be nothing. Life manifests as a polarity which in Genesis is envisaged as spirit hovering over the darkness of the deep, this being the *prima materia*, substance without form which is the Mother aspect. The same patterns repeat themselves throughout the totality of the cosmos, as summed up in the famous Hermetic maxim as above, so below, and, in terms of the human form, this becomes Man and Woman. Thus, the two sexes are based on the fundamental nature of the divine in manifestation which means they should reflect the nature of that dyad. When they do and work together in creative unity, there is love and harmony. When they don't, there results disorder.

God created so that love might find an expressive outlet. He creates humanity as man and woman so that each might be complemented by and fulfilled in the other, and that together they might be more than either on their own or than a self-sufficient androgynous creature would be. There is a theory that life arose androgynously (see Plato, and Eve being formed from Adam's rib) and will evolve back to that as we become 'whole', but this is based on a misunderstanding of why there was creation in the first place. God created to make something more than existed in pure being or oneness. By bringing about separation he creates the possibility of union which means love. There is no love, or certainly not the same sort of love, for an androgynous being because it cannot be completed by its complementary opposite. Life does not evolve to go back to where it was but onwards to ever greater glories.

If androgyny represented some kind of spiritual perfection, we would expect the divine ideal as manifested in Jesus to be like that, but there is no indication that he was. Jesus may have had certain traditionally feminine characteristics, gentleness, compassion, and such like, but these were expressed within the overall context of strong masculinity. It's the same with all highly advanced spiritual people, saints, sages, and mystics. They are not androgynous, even slightly. They are entirely male or female, even though, as developed humans, they are also able to express qualities associated with the opposite sex.

Spiritually speaking, androgyny relates to inner consciousness, not the expression of a being in form. It's a confusion of levels to think it applies to created beings in their outer expression. We are spirit, soul, and body. Spirit, which is being, may be thought to be the same in both sexes, but soul and body, which are our individuality and its outer expression, have sexual qualities being either male or female, not a mix of the two except when things have gone wrong which in a fallen world is always possible.

As earlier stated, some believe human beings are attempting to regain the androgynous state and that explains the confusion of the present day, but the reason for creation was to introduce multiplicity so that love and beauty and goodness could all be positively expressed. To go back to a pre-creation state of oneness takes away the whole point of creation. We should see the androgyne as a symbol of undifferentiated spiritual being and not an actually real thing once creation has occurred. Nor is it a suitable symbol for the end point. For the end is like the beginning in some respects in that unity consciousness is realised, but not like it in others in that differentiation is preserved. That's why creation and evolution make things better than they were in the pre-creation state. We are not aiming to go back to what we were but to advance to something new and higher. There is a purpose to creation, which is to bring difference into undifferentiated being. Yes, we return to inner oneness but a oneness which is expressed in multiple ways through countless individual beings who manifest as either masculine or feminine (as even the Sun and the Moon do) which, in a universe based on polarity, they must. The androgynous state only exists in terms of unmanifested being, but in that state no actual qualities are expressed at all.

The moral of this story is that union is better than oneness.

Male and Female Created He Them

The blurring of the lines between male and female which has been going on for some time now is a spiritual attack on the soul of humanity. Separating us from the reality of nature is the next step on after separating us from the reality of God, and this is one of the best ways to do it because the division between man and woman is fundamental. When you attack nature in this way you attack God who created nature, and you attack him in a more radical way than simply by not believing in him. That, especially in the conditions of the modern world, is often a passive thing, but this is active because it denies the obvious. God is not immediately apparent to human beings as they are in this world. The difference between man and woman is.

Then there is the matter of making us believe lies. We all instinctively know the reality of the two sexes. It is hardwired into us. By making us doubt this reality, by denying it and enforcing that denial through public policy as we do, we acquiesce in a lie and when we accept a lie against what should be our better judgment we have lost our freedom. We become slaves, capitulating to power which is what slavery is. When you believe a lie while inwardly knowing that it is a lie you have handed over your individual integrity to an outside authority and the only authority that you should be doing this to is God. If you do it to anyone or anything else, you are making that thing God. To make people believe palpable nonsense is to control them completely.

Next, this deconstruction of the sexes emasculates men and defeminises women. Everyone loses. Some feeble men might feel safer and more comfortable in such an environment because their weaknesses are pandered to and even portrayed as strengths. Similarly, some power-hungry women might thrive, or think they do, but again this is because their vices now become virtues in the inverted scale of values that have come about. In fact, what is happening is that personal failings are rebranded as positive qualities and encouraged. The spiritual state of such people is dire. They succumb to their faults and there is nothing to bring them back to truth and goodness.

The reasons offered for destroying the boundaries between man and woman are inevitably to do with right-sounding values such as fairness, justice, compassion etc. However, none of these can ever be used as a justification for going against truth. You cannot use secondary values, which they are, to overthrow primary ones, and there is nothing more primary than truth. And to what is the fairness, to what the compassion? The spiritual man or woman, or the earthly one? Reinforcing the fallen earthly man or woman against their spiritual selves is neither just nor compassionate. It is, in fact, quite the reverse because it solidifies them in their fallen state. Jesus did not tell sinners they were fine as they were. He told them to abandon sin and follow him.

If the demons who are behind this attack on the male/ female divide, aided and abetted by their servants, witting and unwitting, in this world, succeed in their aim of destroying masculinity and femininity they will have brought about a situation in which reality is what we want it to be and that means there is no reality. Human beings as they will have become then might have a fake therapeutic spirituality, but they can have no proper spiritual understanding if they reject nature. They will have effectively separated themselves completely from God. This will not be allowed to happen universally, though it may well happen to many individuals. I do see signs of the younger generation, those born in this millennium, beginning to reject the foolishness of their immediate forebears and start to reassert the reality of male and female. I hope this gathers pace. But we have fallen so far it has a long way to go and it may be that only collapse and suffering will bring us back to our senses. It is indeed the character-sapping comforts of the modern world that have brought about the possibility of this lunacy in the first place. In a less artificial environment, it could never have taken off.

God created divisions and boundaries for reasons of knowledge and for reasons of love. It is difference that enables understanding. In an amorphous oneness there is no higher or lower, no better nor worse, no greater nor lesser and therefore nothing can be known. And if a man can become a woman or a woman a man what then of love which, in this sense, is the completing of one soul by the other? Of course there can be love between people of the same sex, but this is not the same as the love between a man and a woman which is profoundly creative as it reflects the union of God and Nature. To seek to destroy the differences between the sexes attacks the root of our being and can only come from something that has so separated itself from God that it has no authentic self. For at the bottom of this being is not goodness, truth, and life but a void, and that is where it seeks to take us.

Sex, believe it or not, is a holy thing. It is precisely because it is a holy thing that it can become a diabolical thing when corrupted. But in itself and when correctly oriented it is love and it is creation. The devil hates it and seeks to despoil it in every way he can either through excess or perversion or else by gelding males and making females barren which seems to be what is behind the latest developments. We must preserve it in its goodness and wholesomeness and allow no deviation from its essential truth.

I got into a conversation recently about whether a transwoman was a woman. When I said no, the two other participants were taken aback by my opinion. It marked me out as a bad or, at least, ignorant and bigoted person. When I asked in what way is such a person, born male but apparently made female by hormone treatment and surgery, a woman, I was told it was what 'she feels herself to be that matters'. In other words, the old feelings trump facts argument. I was told, and it may be true, I don't know, that in some people a female-oriented brain inhabits a male body and so they were clearly female from the beginning. But that is beside the point, I replied. They are in a male body so they are not female. I asked what they thought about the fact that a transwoman would not have a womb or XX chromosomes as a biologically normal woman would have but was told that was irrelevant. Many biologically normal women cannot have children. Are they any less female? No, I said, but a biological woman whose biology is defective is quite different to a biological man who decides to be a woman. I asked if a white person decided he was black did that mean he now was black? They avoided the question, but I fail to see how, in a rational universe, the two cases are different. Perhaps that is the issue here. We no longer live in a rational universe.

I should say that I have the greatest sympathy for anyone who feels him or herself to be born in a body of the wrong sex. This must be a horrible position in which to find oneself, and such people should be treated with compassion. And yet, though medical anomalies do exist, genuine intersex people are rare. Most transexuals are not like this. Moreover, that is not the point. The point is that a society that divorces itself from reality, for whatever reason, is a society that has separated itself from both God and Nature, and it is therefore one that is on the way out. This is just the latest indication that we are such a society.

Having said all this, the whole issue of sexual confusion is one of the characteristics of the end times and further confirmation, if it were needed, that we have indeed entered such a period. In the end times borders are eroded, boundaries breached, and traditions rejected as order and stability are attacked from outside and eaten away from within. This is in line with the general dissolving, dismantling qualities the end times have as the Logos or creative word is no longer heard due to the increasing dominance of the material pole. Demonic forces take advantage of these trends to push their anti-spiritual agenda. They have the wind in their sails at such a time, so to speak, and their influence is harder to resist unless you consciously reach up beyond the material world to the spiritual realm, which is untouched by earthly weather patterns as we might think of these phenomena.

Ultimately, everything is a matter of metaphysics, and to understand what sex really means and how it should work out in the world you have to go right back to the beginning. And the beginning is when the unmanifest One becomes a dyad in order to manifest and bring about Creation. This is the masculine and feminine forces of the universe, known as Siva and Sakti in Tantra where Siva is being, and Sakti, the principle of change. Greek philosophy has a similar sense when it boils reality down to Form or Spirit and Matter. What is not always understood is that it is the masculine principle in its absolute form as the One, or God the Father if you like, that lies behind the manifested dyad, and that it projects a feminine side as its complementary opposite in manifestation. This implies that the feminine to be properly attuned spiritually must love, honour and obey the masculine as in the traditional marriage ceremony, a deeply unpopular idea today. One can see why this would be rejected on the individual level but thinking of it in terms of the immanent obeying the transcendent might make it more palatable to the modern mind and easier to understand. For it is the metaphysical masculine we are talking about here, not the male ego.

Sex does not just exist in the body but in the soul too. In the Golden Age we can assume that men and women were pure representative figures of their Form, but in the Kali Yuga, and especially the tail end of that period, which is the end times, the loss of contact with spirit leads to many instances of a failure to express form in authentic ways. There is also confusion about what men and women are with attempts by each to ape their opposite. This will lead to further separation from the source and a deeper plunge into spiritual darkness because integrity and wholeness can only come about when the outer properly reflects the inner. If the outer tries to express a false inner it separates itself from its true being and causes a breakdown in the structure of the universe or that local part within which the dysfunctional influence operates.

Hierarchy and Complementarity

The two poles of existence of spirit and matter have a dual relationship which is both hierarchical and complementary, and this is echoed in humanity. Complementarity is not the same as equality but has been interpreted as such even by some traditionalists, still partially in thrall to Enlightenment thinking, who decry feminism while saying that men and women are different but equal because they complement each other, with each being superior in its own domain.

That is true as far as it goes but it falls short of the cosmic meaning behind sex differences, and the laws of the macrocosm should be mirrored in the microcosm if order is to prevail on that level. Men and women are certainly complementary to each other. That should be obvious to any rational person, but it does not mean they are equal other than in basic spiritual worth on the individual level. But then they are not unequal either. They are different, and to bring the idea of equality into this relationship is to confuse what exists in qualitative terms with the quantitative.

The reality is that there is a hierarchical as well as a complementary aspect to the masculine/feminine polarity which is symbolised in the story that Eve came out of Adam's side not vice versa. It is also shown by the fact that to God all souls are feminine in respect of their relationship to him. He represents the positive pole. The nature of masculinity and femininity finds its first origins in this relationship. A Christian might see it reflected in the idea that the church is the bride of Christ. This is a relationship of love but not equality which in this context is a foreign concept introduced where it does not belong in response to Enlightenment influence which interprets the spiritual in terms of the material.

To say that men and women are complementary and equal but different with women better at being women and men better at being men is true, but it is not the whole truth. Regarding the second part of that statement, you could say the same thing about human beings and butterflies. The fact is that to frame this relationship in terms of equality *or* inequality is mistaken. The metaphysical position is that the positive/masculine pole is prior in the order of creation, and, in that sense, it is the masculine that has spiritual authority. But each pole is unique, and the feminine is an essential part of creation which is necessarily dualistic as in subject and object, and it stands to the masculine as matter does to spirit. Without matter spirit cannot be expressed but spirit is the primordial reality. This foundation truth lies at the heart of the masculine/feminine polarity, and in a smooth-running universe it should function with love and creativity. But in the fallen human world male misuse of power and female striving for power has created a war between the sexes. Not to mention a lack of love on both sides. This is all summed up by Julius Evola in his book *Eros and the Mysteries of Love*, where he writes that *the natural and unchangeable law rooted in the very metaphysics of male and female is "reciprocal integration and completion together with a subordination of the female principle to the male."* We normally only focus on one or other of those two aspects of the law, but both go together to make the whole of it, and if one is not observed then the law is not being observed.

The hierarchical aspect to the relationship does not mean that women should merely be submissive wives and mothers as in some traditional Christian schools of thought. Still less does it support the Islamic fear and suppression of women which has only produced a stunted and largely uncreative culture in which the principle of law totally dominates that of love. That overemphasises one side of Evola's law and ignores the other. Furthermore, in our day the change in consciousness, entailing a greater focus on the self, that started in the West and then spread everywhere, affected everyone, men and women, and this impacts all traditional expressions of the law. But the female expression of that change in consciousness should be within the context of womanhood not pseudo-masculinity, and it must still observe the priority of the masculine pole. There will be individual cases where that is not so, but these are the exceptions that prove the rule. In general, the principle of masculine or solar rulership must hold if culture and civilisation are to function according to spiritual principles. When it does not everything will fall apart as is beginning to happen in our day, whether admitted or not.

God has given us the sun and the moon to demonstrate the truth of this relationship. The sun rules the day and the moon the night and, in that sense, they are complementary, one to the other. But the moon draws its light from the sun though it processes this light according to its own unique nature. Esoterically, there are lunar mysteries where the feminine rules and solar mysteries where it is the masculine force that dominates. But the solar mysteries relate to higher initiations and deeper truths, spirit rather than soul. Early man worshipped the Great Mother or Goddess because he only knew the natural and psychic worlds, and could not yet relate to higher spiritual forces. Spiritual evolution in those days consisted of breaking free of the bond of the mother which was essential if man was to become a free agent, and there are many stories in early mythology that relate to this battle. Now, we live in an era in which the feminine is rightly reasserting itself after a period of suppression, but it is doing so in an unbalanced way. The feminine must be expressed but it must be so in the context of wisdom rather than desire for power, which means it must recognise the overall rulership of the masculine, using the word overall because there are certainly areas where the feminine rules – see the comment above regarding the moon. Men and women complement each other, of course they do, but there is no such thing as equality anywhere in the universe. It is a doctrine spread by the fallen powers in an attempt to put their agenda on an equal footing with that of God.

The goal of evolution is the complete infusion of matter by spirit with its subsequent transformation and glorification. This is the mystic marriage of cosmic masculine and cosmic feminine which foreshadows the union of God with his creation. Thus, we can see that the feminine, which is matter, nature, all creation, and the masculine, which is spirit, are two halves of one whole. In a horizontal sense equal because both need each other but in the vertical sense spirit has hierarchical pre-eminence.

This is a teaching that is both simple and complicated. Simple because it is what is. Therefore, it is stamped into our very being. It is natural to us when we are correctly oriented and alive to reality. But it is complicated too because we live in a world that has lost touch with its origins, and we ourselves are dominated by our egos, our desires, fears, and ambitions. The female ego resents male authority while the male ego abuses that authority for its own ends. Both need to realise that this authority is not for the benefit of the male but for the benefit of the whole. Moreover, it is meant to function under the overall authority of God. In the past the masculine head has been turned by power, power sought for personal ends, so it was inevitable that there would be a reaction and a rebellion against a corrupted state when human consciousness had progressed from a group-oriented stage to the more self-centred one which it has done over the course of the last few centuries. But the corruption of a natural thing does not mean the thing itself is wrong, only that the corrupting elements should be purged, and there should be a return to origins.

And yet, not quite a return to origins, for the development of consciousness does mean that the relationship between men and women should incorporate evolutionary advancements whilst expressing those within the context of universal spiritual truth. Therefore, it does not return to exactly what it was but progresses to reflect the earlier state in a new form on a higher turn of the spiral.

The Bhagavata Purana is a collection of writings dedicated to the god Vishnu and his incarnation as Krishna, which, in written form, dates to the second half of the first millennium AD. Its final section contains extensive prophecies about the Kali Yuga and the general decline of humanity that takes place then which includes atheism, secularism, worship of money, and general immoral behaviour. One of the verses specifically states that *"women will try to become independent of the protection of men,"* and another that *"In Kali-yuga men will be wretched and controlled by women."* The rebellion of the female sex against the male is one of the prime markers of the end times in several other traditions, and might be expected at a time when the material pole starts to dominate as the degradation of the cosmic environment obscures spirit. The fact it is to be expected does not make it right but does confirm it to be part of the universal loss of connection to the centre. One more sign among many that humanity as a collective has severed its moorings from reality.

No More Sea

Even though we live in an age of individualism, or maybe because of it, many people in these end times seem to find selfhood a burden they would like to discard. This explains some of the attraction to Buddhist doctrines and forms of so-called oneness spirituality. Freud described the sensation sought here as the 'oceanic feeling', meaning the feeling that one is dissolved into something larger, be it humanity, the cosmos, or a pantheistic god. In contrast to this return to amorphousness where the burdens of existence are lifted from one's shoulders but the positive joys are too, Christianity offers a relationship to God that does not dissolve the self. The self is radically transfigured, but it is not destroyed.

Interestingly, this might be seen as a basic difference at first principles level between left and right. For the spiritual leftist the ideal is to lose oneself by reducing everything to nothing, whereas for the integrated man on the right, as for the enlightened Christian, spirituality is a matter of finding one's self. This is egalitarianism and freedom taken to their logical conclusions, and points to the fact that the roots of egalitarianism may lie in the desire to return to the pre-created state by eliminating distinctions rather than upholding justice as usually claimed. Creation is differentiation which gets more not less as it unfolds and develops, which suggests it might be fear that motivates both the search for the oceanic state and, by extension, egalitarian ideology itself, absorption into undivided oneness being an easier, less challenging option than transforming the self through love.

The oceanic feeling is a real thing, but as drugs and even mental illness can bring it about its value in real spiritual terms is questionable. I would describe it as consciousness slipping outside the boundaries of the solid core of the rational self and becoming temporarily reabsorbed in the universal substance from which individualised consciousness is drawn, but that is like the self returning to the spiritual womb rather than growing up and becoming transfigured, in the process retaining individuality but expanding that into divine being. Which is why I would say that the oceanic feeling constitutes a return to the past.

This marine phrase was used by Freud as a psychological (i.e. nonreligious) description of religious experience, but in fact it was the French writer Romain Rolland who came up with the term, and he introduced it to Freud. Rolland coined the phrase to describe the feelings of being one with the universe and of time being taken up into eternity that he read about in his studies of Indian mysticism, particularly from the life of the 19th century Bengali mystic Ramakrishna who frequently experienced spiritual raptures.

Ramakrishna is an appealing figure because of his childlike innocence and transparent goodness, and he might be said to be one of the main sources for the Western discovery of Indian mysticism through his disciple Swami Vivekananda. He was certainly a genuine saint in the Indian tradition. However, his experiences have been diagnosed as possibly caused by temporal lobe epilepsy, which puts them in a slightly different light to that in which they are normally perceived which is as the ecstasies of an enlightened mystic. It also raises the possibility that the search for higher consciousness in this earthly life, which is what lies behind many Westerners' attraction to Eastern mysticism, may be something of a red herring. Ramakrishna was the first Indian mystic of recent times to be seen as living in a state of heightened spiritual reality. If this state was actually or partially a result of mental illness, we must ask ourselves if the approach to the spiritual path that sees it as a search for higher consciousness may, in fact, be a mistaken one. This is neither to deny the reality of higher states of consciousness nor of Ramakrishna's spiritual attainment, which was demonstrated in other ways, but maybe higher consciousness in this life is not what the spiritual search should be aiming at. Traditionally, higher states of consciousness were regarded as completely incidental to proper spiritual practice and sometimes even positively misleading. We are meant to learn the lessons of this world whilst in this world, not to try to escape to a higher one, tempting as that might be.

I am not generally an enthusiast for the theories of Freud who seems to me a typical 19th century materialist in many respects. When I first heard of the Oedipus complex, I thought it the complete nonsense it is. However, some of his work on dreams and the unconscious and the various drives that determine human motivation was valuable at the time even if it is outdated now. And what he apparently thought about the oceanic feeling is also worth considering. He envisaged it as the reversion to a pre-ego state, something experienced by the infant before it becomes aware of self and other. That idea is similar to the one I mention above which postulates that the mystical sense of oneness in which the ego is blotted out is a reflection of the pre-incarnation state when the soul is bathed in the bliss of non-separation. Thus, it is not where we should be headed but where we are coming from, and that means that attempts to recapture it are misguided. No doubt, it will be recapitulated at a later stage once the lessons of incarnation have been learnt, but that will mean expanding the sense of individuality into divine being not contracting it to nothing. The oceanic feeling is entirely passive whereas we are intended by God to be co-creators with him, and that means able to wield divine powers for the benefit of all creation. The soul submerged in the oceanic feeling remains inert. We are meant to be eagles not fish.

The Book of Revelation is a foundation text from the point of view of end times theory. Often interpreted, never fully understood, it remains an enigma but a fascinating one. I am not going to join the ranks of the would-be interpreters, but I would like to consider a few phrases which have a bearing on our present subject. The first comes from Revelation 21:1: *"And I saw a new heaven and a new earth, for the first heaven and the first earth were passed away, and there was no more sea."* The second reference is in Revelation 4:6 where it says: *"Before the throne there was as it were a sea of glass, like crystal"*; and then a bit further on we have Revelation 15:2 with, *"I saw what appeared to be a sea of glass mingled with fire, and those who had conquered the beast and its image and the number of its name stand on the sea of glass with harps from God."*

These extracts refer to the end of time when good has finally driven all evil from the world and the spiritual journey is complete. Creation is taken up into God as the New Jerusalem descends. However, the two references are a little different. The first is a factual statement. There is no more sea. The second doesn't seem to be meant literally. It alludes to something that looks like a sea of glass ('as it were', 'what appeared to be') but is possibly not actually such. The image may just be used comparatively. Nevertheless, I think they are referring to a similar phenomenon and one that manifests on both the material and spiritual levels, because at this stage in the proceedings these two have become one in the sense that the outer is now a perfect representation of the inner. The Fall has been reversed and time has fulfilled its purpose so that it conjoins with eternity to create something new.

What does the sea symbolise? It is the primeval ocean from which life emerges once it has been fertilised by the spirit of God moving on the face of the waters. It is chaos and formlessness, and it is darkness and deep which are the symbols of origin. We know now what the writer of Genesis could not have known, that life started in the sea and only emerged onto dry land once it had reached a certain state of development. But it's all there in Genesis.

The sea is potential. It is the undifferentiated oneness from which life is formed once it has been impregnated by the Word of God. Hence, no more sea means that potential has been actualised. That which began in the Mother has been born, reached maturity, and gone on to the Father. To return to the sea is to return to the infantile state of the child one with the Mother. It is to lose freedom by returning to formlessness.

In a psychological sense the sea is also the subconscious, that in which monsters lurk but also a source of imagination and creativity when illumined by the Logos. No more sea from this point of view means no more subconscious and that means that the individual, or, at the end of time, the whole human race, has become fully conscious. There are no dark hidden corners in consciousness. Everything has been irradiated by light. The body itself has become light. Occultists talk of the astral plane which is made up of the thoughts, desires, fears, aspirations, and so on of humanity but a spiritually ignorant humanity separate from God. It is regarded as a vale of illusion even if it contains beauty. This astral plane is also the sea and for the disciple risen with Christ it ceases to exist, being replaced by that of which it is a man-made distortion which is the quality of love/wisdom.

The sea, then, is the ground of manifested existence, both physically and psychologically. No more sea means that the journey of evolving life is complete, and I would say that the sea of glass points to a similar reality. In the second of the two references it is mingled with fire which suggests divine love. Watery love implies something soft and weak, a generalised state of sentimental concern with feelings. But fiery love is intense, creative, genuinely passionate. The sea of glass symbolises emotions controlled, mastered, stilled. The saints stand on it so they can use it, but they are not submerged in it, and the fire shows that unstable, changeable human emotions have been transformed into divine love.

Perhaps the whole evolutionary journey is to make water into light. Life must start in the waters which contain the nourishment to make God's thoughts grow. From its depths life emerges onto dry land but then the next stage is to take flight and go through the air up to fire which is the light of God. Could we say that our current refusal to accept the reality of spirit is a refusal to take the next stage of leaving the hard material earth and soar up to the sky, figuratively speaking? Some of us want to return to the sea where we will only drown. Some want to stay on the physical earth, but God is calling us to mount up to the heavens.

Some of the observations in this chapter were inspired by remarks made by Professor J.M. Smith and Lady Mermaid.

Part Four

Spiritual Practice

Spiritual Routine

You might think these two words have nothing in common. One suggests love, beauty, mystery, glory, the undiscovered country. The other seems dull, boring, workaday, uncreative, unimaginative. One is a mystic on a mountaintop. The other is a clerk in an office. However, as far as life in this world is concerned, they do belong together.

When one starts on the spiritual path in any serious sense one is full of enthusiasm (literal meaning, possessed by a god) for the journey ahead. Great vistas seem to open up and life has the promise of moving into more and more magnificence. For a newcomer to the path the world can seem irradiated by light, suffused with new meaning. We are often impelled to this new life, which truly can seem like being reborn, by an experience of some sort which temporarily lifts the veil between this world and the next. We imagine this is just the beginning of a glorious journey.

And so it is. But this journey can be a long, hard slog. The excitement of early days may soon dissipate as the reality of the spiritual path kicks in. For the path is not about higher states of consciousness or bliss or happiness in this life. It is about work. The work required to make your soul a fit receptacle for God. The cleaning, polishing work, the removal of dust, dirt, and deeply engrained stains work, the work required to address bad habits of a lifetime (or of lifetimes). It is to do with knowing yourself and facing up to facts about yourself you may not like and which you suppress. The path has the habit of unearthing all that and confronting you with the reality of what you are which is good because you can't get into heaven with any darkness in your soul. You can't cheat God.

The routine of spiritual life is what is required for the work you need to do on yourself. My teachers told me over 40 years ago that my life would continue in a routine until I left my physical body. Such has been and continues to be the case. There is nothing glamorous about proper spiritual work. Of course, there can be moments of upliftment, but we come to Earth to work and get to grips with what holds us back from deeper engagement with the source of life and divine being. Here is the perfect environment for that. But most of the time it is not exciting so don't expect it to be. In fact, if it is you should probably ask yourself what has gone wrong. Have you been led off the path by some temptation to the lower self, that self that is always looking for gratification of some kind?

Monks used to be warned that if they received too much what was called spiritual consolation or divine sweetness, what we nowadays might refer to as higher states of consciousness, visions, ecstasies, and the like, it could well be the demonic forces rather than God that were bestowing these. You can be a spiritual libertine as well as a sensual one and this was the trap that many New Age enthusiasts, or those who looked to the East or to some exotic guru for enlightenment, fell into. You become a spiritual pleasure seeker and forget that what is really required is sanctification of the soul, and this demands self-abnegation, acceptance of discipline, humility, and hard work. The rewards are greater than we can conceive of, but they are not in this life, which is about preparation for the feast not the feast itself.

Why would we come to the physical world if there was not work to be done here? There is no point in having spiritual experiences all the time in this world because that denies us the opportunity to work on ourselves. Why bother if we are not driven to it by a sense of something missing? Spiritual experiences may come but they are usually like carrots to lead the donkey which is why they are more common for novices than for those established on the path, often to the disappointment of the latter who may have thought that initial experiences were the precursor to something more. However, a little reflection should show that such occurrences, if too frequent, would only feed the ego in most cases. God wants those who love him for himself not for his gifts, and so he withdraws his gifts in order that we may learn to become what previously we have only experienced.

Given the anti-spiritual nature of the end times, it is important to establish good spiritual habits that will counteract the prevailing psychic tendencies. This is best done through regular discipline and routine, though one must avoid the potential boredom and monotony such practices might engender after a while by constantly making efforts to keep things fresh through full engagement. Spiritual development has always required swimming against the current of one's own egotism and sheer laziness because it does demand a substantial effort to sustain. Now to those are added another obstructive force which is a heavily materialised atmosphere and environment. To do this successfully requires the support of a solid routine.

We have mentioned before that the end times are in part the product of the law of entropy. Matter is only maintained in order by the action of spirit. Left to itself it descends into the chaos that is its raw state. Entropic decay leads eventually to the end times which represent that period at the conclusion of a cycle when the creative forces of spirit are running low because they are so far distant from their originating impulse and source. They are still present, or the environment would disintegrate completely, but they are less dominant. The result of this entropy produces both perversion and inversion of spiritual truth as perceived in the human mind which is the reason for that alarming prophecy in Matthew 24, *"For there shall arise false Christs, and false prophets, who shall show great signs and wonders; insomuch that, if it were possible, they shall deceive the very elect."*

Jesus is saying that even the most spiritually attentive can be led astray by the corruption in the latter days. He describes these people as the elect by which he means those who are alive today to counteract end times collapse from the inside. However, once incarnate they too will be subject to the prevailing forces, and may as a result forget their mission or be led away from fulfilling it correctly. In a broader sense, anyone who seeks to hold fast to the truth and maintain spiritual integrity is part of the elect. We would all like to think we belong among this group, but we should do well to remember that we are tested where we are weakest and even the elect can fall. We might resist one illusion but then be deceived by something coming from the opposite direction. We may be impervious to some assaults on truth but still succumb to something that plays on our weaknesses. Right motivation is essential on the spiritual path. It will not protect us from everything, we must have right discernment too, but it will guide us through many difficulties and enable us to resist many temptations. Establishing a strong spiritual routine will help with this.

To be part of the elect is not a glamorous position. Their role is to serve and quite possibly to suffer too for the suffering of the saints is a kind of expiation for the whole of humanity. They will not be thanked or acclaimed or rewarded. They may even be condemned as their Master was but then the mark of the elect is that they seek only to tread the path of light in truth and love, come what may. If we would join them, we must have that attitude too.

A proper spiritual routine which correctly orients one to divine truth is one of the surest ways to protect oneself against end times deception.

Illusion and Sin

There are two approaches to the spiritual path. They are markedly different which indicates that the real path should incorporate them both. However, many people opt for one and ignore the other or else pay the other only a token acknowledgement. In the case of the second approach this is limiting but not necessarily a spiritual problem. In the case of the first, it can indeed be a problem. It seems that this first approach is becoming more popular these days, and part of the reason for that is because it appeals more to the desire for power, spiritual power, personal power, or just general self-expansion which latter term would include the expansion of consciousness (see earlier chapter). Desire for power motivates us all whether we admit to it or not. This is actually a good thing at root because we are meant to grow and increase, but it becomes unhealthy when taken over by the ego or fallen self.

I wonder if the devil and his fellow fallen angels are really in hell. What I mean by this is to question whether these beings are subject to permanent pain, torture, and suffering as would traditionally be the case for the denizens of hell. I would speculate that many spiritually fallen souls do indeed experience these privations but the higher-ranking beings in what C.S. Lewis wittily called the Lowerarchy may not. At least, they may not in the way we think. They will certainly suffer the loss of the proximity to God and be deprived in that respect, but they may have means of anaesthetising this loss through artificial means rather as drugs can be painkillers. The devil can bestow the sensation of an expanded consciousness on human beings and by so doing lead them to thinking he is an angel of light. This is why one should always treat any supposed spiritual experience with circumspection. Does it foster love and humility, or does it lead to inflation? If the devil can do this to humans, then it is reasonable to assume he can concoct such states for himself. He was, after all, a great angel. He has lost much but not everything. He has lost God but not what he was himself or not all of it anyway. Demons steal spiritual energy, this is what keeps them in existence since they can no longer receive it directly from God, and they can use this to give themselves false spiritual light. This is a large part of the reason they attack humanity, to absorb an energy they cannot absorb directly. The devil suffers on the true spiritual level, but he may experience an elevated consciousness simply by virtue of what he is. He is a thief, and he can steal spiritual goods though he can never hold on to them.

The reason for this digression is to illustrate the potential problems with one of the two approaches I mentioned earlier, the one I said is becoming more popular partly because of the power aspect but also because it draws the intellectual type of seeker who regards himself as halfway divine already. Jesus said we are gods, but the devil also said that in his guise as the serpent in the Garden of Eden. There are gods and there are gods. There are gods in Christ and there are gods outside of Christ. Choose carefully which one you want to be. To be a god in Christ means to let Christ into your heart. You become a god through him. To be a god outside of Christ means to seek to become a god in your own right. You are divine. Godhood is your right because you already are God. Or so the story goes. This is the created being seeking to usurp the rights of the Creator. These rights are not yours but can only be bestowed by grace.

The two spiritual paths are illusion to enlightenment and sin to repentance. Many people today prefer the first because it asks less of them. They will admit that enlightenment requires the giving up of ego, but they think this just means seeing through the impermanence or transience or illusionary nature of the ego state which fades away by itself in meditation or when higher states of consciousness are reached. Not so. Giving up ego is not an intellectual exercise nor is the fallen self something that you just 'see through'. It requires genuine self-sacrifice and repentance of sin to defeat the ego. So much sin is unacknowledged by the seekers of enlightenment because they regard sin as part of illusion. It is not or, if it is, it is much more than simple ignorance. We live in a state of sin because we are fallen. No amount of wisdom or enlightenment will change that. It must be renounced through full repentance. This is the only water that washes away the stain of sin from the human heart. The seekers of enlightenment may attain higher states of consciousness, spiritual power of a sort, and great knowledge. They will not attain union with God or entry into heaven unless they repent their sins. And their spiritual accomplishments may well lead them deeper into sin if they are not careful. The devil doesn't just trap people with material wealth and power. He can also trap them with spiritual wealth and power. It is only the recognition that you are a sinner and repentance that can defeat him.

Those seeking enlightenment need to understand that they are sinners and the full implication of what that means. You cannot become divine merely by recognising your own true nature. You are potentially divine but can only become truly so as a gift from God, and that gift is only bestowed on those who fully abandon their fallen self in repentance. This is an ongoing process, but God looks for the sincere heart and rewards that accordingly.

To point to the potential flaws in the search for enlightenment does not mean that search is wrong so far as it goes. It is very necessary to see through illusion and to strive for higher understanding. But let this be done by the soul dedicated to Christ, one that recognises that any divinity we might acquire comes not from within ourselves but in and through him.

A concern with personal sinfulness is regarded as spiritually old-fashioned in some quarters because it is associated with a theistic approach to truth, which is regarded as on a lower level than the non-dualistic one in which there is no intrinsic difference between human and divine consciousness, as the former is the latter in its essence. This is the mistake made by those who restrict God to immanence and neglect his transcendence. In reality, both are real. It might be seen as yet another sign of the end times that so many seek the benefits of spirituality without acknowledging the one from whom those benefits flow or being prepared to make the sacrifices required, chief of which is the recognition that one is a sinner in need of salvation. This requires a far deeper engagement with the roots of self than simply dismissing them as illusion.

The greatest saints see themselves as great sinners. They accept that their lives may be filled with suffering and spiritual darkness when God withdraws completely from them in order to purge them of their sin. It is interesting to read that the writings of St. Thérèse of Lisieux were altered before publication to reflect a more saccharine ideal of piety in line with 19th century sentimentality. In fact, she experienced many spiritual trials and even the loss of faith which are related in her *Story of a Soul.* She speaks of travelling through a dark tunnel from which she had not come out and feeling that she lived in a country covered by a thick fog while longing for the beautiful land that was her true home. *"When I sing of the happiness of heaven,"* she writes, *"I feel no joy in this. I sing simply what I want to believe."* But then she goes on to say with a wisdom that belies her youth that she understands why God did not send this trial until he knew she could bear it. She realises that her suffering is God's greatest gift to her because in cleansing her of sin it is preparing her soul for heaven.

Empathy and Love

We live in an age in which empathy is regarded as a highly desirable characteristic, but can you have too much empathy? Most people would agree you can have too little, but can you have too much? A moment's reflection should tell us that yes, obviously, you can. If empathy is not balanced by intelligence and wisdom or just common sense, it will become destructive. If it is not coupled with discernment, a sense of justice, and a love of truth it may well do more harm than good.

This is true even insofar as real empathy is concerned. How much truer it is for the fake empathy we have these days. Jesus said in Matthew 9:5–8, "*When you pray, do not be like the hypocrites, for they love to pray standing in the synagogues and on the street corners to be seen by men ... but when you pray, go into your room, close the door and pray to your father who is unseen.*" The hypocrites here are like the modern empathisers who display their empathy to feel good about themselves and show off their virtue. This is hardly news. It is human nature, or a symptom of the fallen part of it, and just takes new forms. The underlying character weakness remains the same.

But let's forget about that and assume all empathisers feel real empathy. Unless this emotion, for that is what it is, is counterbalanced by proper discernment it simply opens the door to exploitation. A culture that overemphasises empathy will be destroyed because it lacks a functioning immune system. It will allow anything to enter its body without discriminating between the good and the bad, the healthy and the sick, the nutritious and the poisonous. To the pathologically empathetic this will sound wicked and cruel, but in the real world we need wisdom as much as innocence and sometimes a supposed innocence is an excuse for evading moral responsibility.

It can be pleasant to feel empathy but to a certain psychological type it is an indulgence, a wallowing in sentiment. The demands of life require steel as well as silk, and a virtue exaggerated or exercised without its complement becomes a vice, one the devil well knows how to exploit for his own ends.

Empathy is not love but it becomes mistaken for it when you have lost the love of God.

And we have lost the love of God. As a result, we have no idea what love is, which is why we come up with such banal statements as love is love. If ever there was a cliché suited to the prevailing mentality of the end times when qualitative truth is undermined by egalitarian priorities, then this is it. Love may be love, but what is love? I once heard someone claim that God had told him there was complete moral equivalence between homosexuality and heterosexuality because we are all evolving into a state in which sex (meaning gender as we say nowadays) will not exist. On a certain level this idea might seem persuasive, but it is a misconception.

The only place that sex, as in masculine and feminine or their initiating equivalents on the metaphysical level, cannot exist is the unmanifest state, the one in which spirit and matter are not yet sundered and nothing is. The very act of creation involves a division which, whether you call it consciousness and form, spirit and matter, or God and Nature, is the root of the sex difference in man. That goes right down to the ground of reality in that for creation to take place, one must become two. If you don't want sex to exist, then you don't want life to exist.

A rejoinder to this might be that we will all become androgynous but, as we have already discussed, that is a category error in that it forces a pre-manifested condition into the world of manifestation which word I use here as an equivalent for creation even if they are somewhat different, metaphysically speaking. But if life is to be expressed there must be this duality of subject and object and that, right there, is the sex difference. It cannot be dispensed with if life is to be experienced as anything more than pure consciousness. Even to be conscious of something requires a duality, and that is the ground from which masculine and feminine grow.

It may be that as humanity evolves the sexes will become more refined in their form and expression, and some might confuse this as each of them becoming more like the other, but the unique categories of masculine and feminine will remain and, in fact, become more what they are in absolute terms as they approach that level. But they will also include attributes of their complementary opposite though framed in the context of their own nature which is always primary. In Luke chapter 13 God is compared to a hen who gathers her brood under her wings but that does not make him any less God the Father. Great men can have great compassion, but they are no less men. Great women can have a strong will, but they are no less women. One androgynous being can never complement and complete another androgynous being, and it is this completing and complementing that makes the love between man and woman what it is. Apart from being a necessity for creation, the sexual division of beings is a great gift from God because it takes love to a new level.

Love is love but what people often mean when they say this is that love is sex. They smuggle in one thing by claiming it is another. Love is indeed love if it is pure and does not degenerate, but most of what is called love by propagandists is degenerated love that arises from and is intended to satisfy the ego not the soul.

A truth ignored by Christianity is the pre-existence of the soul. I believe in reincarnation though whether it is for everyone or only some I couldn't say. The background to life in this world is more complicated than we know. But reincarnation or not, no human soul born here is a new creation. We all come from somewhere, and while we do not necessarily share the same originating source as souls have different spiritual backgrounds, we all have a pre-existing soul before taking birth in the material world. This incarnating soul is neither sexless nor androgynous. It is either masculine or feminine, though bear in mind that the soul is our individual consciousness and at a deeper level of being there is the divine spark that is God in us. The idea that our spiritual selves have no sex is an elevation of abstract theory to truth, and a rejection of the beauty of creation for a retreat into an idealised non-being. That said, it is possible for male souls to be born into female bodies and vice versa but this does not justify current approaches because if they are so born it is to learn particular lessons. To avoid these lessons is to waste an opportunity, not to mention put one's own personal will above that of God and try to force reality to one's own desire.

Compassion and truth must go together, taking account of one another if disorder is to be avoided. To focus on one to the detriment of the other leads to imbalance which is why the wise seek to satisfy the demands of both. Yet there is still a hierarchy to this relationship for it is compassion that should balance truth not the other way round.

What Is Evil?

Understanding the nature of the battle between good and evil is fundamental to successfully negotiating the end times. After all, if you don't know what evil is then you will not be able to resist it, and you must resist it in the sense of identify and stand against it even if you should not respond to it by allowing it to drag you down by your reaction to it. See it, know it, reject it, but do not react to it inwardly. That is the formula.

The battle is ongoing, but something distinguishes the present from any previous time. For while everyone recognises material evil, comparatively few in our day understand what spiritual evil is, and that is the greater of the two in that it affects the soul rather than the body.

What, then, is evil in the spiritual sense? The answer is simple. Evil is the rejection of God. This rejection may show itself in different ways but these all spring from the same refusal to acknowledge the Creator. And the rejection of God is also the rejection of goodness because God is goodness. This means that a person who rejects God supports evil, not in the everyday sense but in the spiritual. I realise this is a controversial position to take but the fact is that if you deny God, you will do bad things from the spiritual point of view.

Perhaps at one time there were legitimate grounds for doubting the reality of God. Human consciousness had changed, and a religion formed for the previous stage of consciousness was no longer sufficient for many even if the basics were still present. But now anyone of good faith should be able to see where the rejection of God has taken us and where it will take us in the future if it continues. This should force any agnostic or atheist to reassess his position. A period of doubt is inevitable for most people in the modern world and is even healthy as it can lead to a deeper faith as one reconsiders the nature of life, the self, and the world, and no longer takes religion on face value but penetrates beneath its surface. But that period should not be a destination. The healthy soul will move on to acceptance of divine truth.

Why do I say this so confidently? Partly because God is in us and he will speak to us if we do not suppress his voice, and partly because a healthy soul seeks love, goodness, and beauty, and these cannot exist unless they are grounded in a God. Otherwise, they are no more real than the appearance of a face formed by clouds. They become utilitarian which means they only have an existence of convenience so can be replaced at any time. So, either you accept these things are not real in which case anything goes, or else you acknowledge their reality in which case you must acknowledge the existence of that which gives them reality.

Where has this rejection of God taken us? For a start, it has taken us to a world of post-truth. This had been creeping up on us for decades, but it took over around the turn of the millennium since when everything is said and done for appearance and effect. Very little simply because it is right. Recently we have seen that even science has become more a matter of consensus than truth, and as for politics, the least said the better.

Then it has taken us to the triumph of technology. Technology starts as the attempt to force Nature to human will which implies the prioritising of matter over spirit, but then as it proceeds and develops it becomes the means to remake the human form, changing it from being in the image of God to a self-created thing which, by definition, is a deformed thing.

All the various ideologies of the modern world which are supposedly humanistic are really Satanic. They are so because they reject God and try to recreate not only human society but even the human being (see above) in a form that has no need of God. The only conclusion to be drawn from this really quite obvious fact is that modernism, the whole of it not just the more extreme parts, is evil. If that shocks you or seems excessive it is only because the full effects of the modernistic agenda have not yet been realised. But the steps that lead to that end certainly have. One leads to another and on we go to the inevitable conclusion though maybe there is no clear end, just a deeper and darker descent into spiritual loss and separation. In fact, there will be an end because God will not permit things to progress beyond a certain point, but there is some way to go as most people are not yet fully corrupted.

To say that the whole of modernism is evil refers to its manifestation in today's world. It does not mean there was nothing good or necessary about the developments in human consciousness that came about in the Western world from where they spread all over the globe. This was a spiritual advance but the energies behind it were captured and perverted by demonic forces, and the new sense of self-awareness instead of dedicating itself to pursuing divine mysteries became fixated on itself. God was rejected and into that vacant spot humanity put itself, though it will find that what it has really done is made itself the dupe of said demonic forces. Now we have reached the point where to retain any aspect of modernism in any of the various forms that have come down to us is like not cutting out a canker from a plant. It will spread over the whole plant, corrupting and killing it. Everything that the world believes today must be reassessed in the light of the reality of God and his purpose for the soul.

Can I really be saying here that people who don't believe in God are bad people? Don't we all have friends and family who do not believe yet who are good, decent people, not to mention those who do but are not? That is not the point. For a start, many people think they believe in God but just subscribe to an image and are not awake in the heart which is where true belief is centred. This is what I am talking about here. A simple test to distinguish between the two is to ask if you see the world in the light of God or God in the light of the world.

Then there is the further point that this is not about personal behaviour. It has to do with whether the heart is open to the source of truth and goodness. A heart that is so open is a good heart and will acknowledge God. One that is not so open is rejecting the source of goodness. How can you call that good? So, you see, it is not about whether you are good which in the modern world means relatively tolerant and charitable and not much more, but whether you love good, actively love real spiritual good. Those who do will believe in God because one inevitably means the other. Those who don't love good will not believe in God. It's all about love. Genuine believers in God may behave badly. They shouldn't, but they may. We are, after all, all sinners, and repentance is an ongoing requirement. Those who reject God may lead outwardly exemplary lives but that is of little matter if their heart is turned away from their Creator. I repeat it is all to do with whether the heart is actively oriented to real goodness. This need not take the same outer form in all cases. Many spiritual approaches contain pathways to God, even if Christ remains the Way, the Truth, and the Life, and ultimately no one comes to the Father except through him. But people take different ways to get to him, and his spirit can manifest in different religions in hidden form. Perhaps elsewhere than in conventional religions too. Many true-hearted people who have their own traditions cannot accept Christianity because it is too associated with alien ideology and power. Others cannot because it is too contaminated by its worldly forms. God will certainly not leave such people without a witness to his presence.

I know an atheist who believes nothing that has not been confirmed by science. Talking about the transsexual trend of recent years he said he will wait for science to pronounce until making up his mind on the reality or otherwise of genuinely being able to change sex. A young man who was present at this conversation asked, "What about basic common sense? We don't need science to corroborate that." "We certainly do," said the atheist. "Nothing can be regarded as true until scientifically proven to be so. What is called common sense cannot be relied upon."

This individual represents a typical kind of modern person who has so separated himself from reality, both objective reality and the reality of himself as a human being, that he doubts everything and sees meaning in nothing. This is the result of rejecting the primary fact of a Supreme Being who gives reality and meaning to everything. He is reducing himself to a thin-souled being of less and less substance. He is wasting away spiritually. A clairvoyant might see him as surrounded by a hard shell which blocks out any incoming light. It is a sorry state to be in and requires a big turnaround of consciousness to escape a self-created prison of this sort. C.S. Lewis in his novel *The Great Divorce* has a character like this who, transported to the heavenly world, refuses to accept it for fear of being tricked, and shrinks down to near-nothingness in consequence.

Doubtless many people during the Nazi rise to power turned a blind eye to moral evil, But now the situation is not so very different. Most of the Western population turn a blind eye to spiritual evil and so become complicit in its spread. These people are not outwardly evil, but by not standing against it, they become part of it and their souls are damaged. When the end times arrive, neutrality is not an option. Jesus says in Matthew 12:30: *"Whoever is not with me is against me, and whoever does not gather with me scatters."* There are many who scatter in the present day simply because they do not gather.

At one time I considered the mystical path to be the proper end for every human soul. I still do. The spiritual light must be kindled and burst into flames within the heart. However, we are not just called to a union with God where we transcend the vicissitudes of this world which is then regarded as a vale of illusion. We must also actively fight spiritual evil as Jesus did, and to do that we must be able to recognise it. Spiritual evil is subtle and will pose as good, worldly good, good for the fallen human being, utopian good, and many spiritual approaches of the present day can be co-opted into spiritual evil because they do not actively stand out against it. Not to recognise good and evil in the world, either because everything is one or the world is a limited state in which nothing is truer than anything else, is not spiritually advanced but moral relativism, and moral relativism plays into the hands of the dark powers who will corrupt the minds of those who do not actively reject them and all they promote.

Give Them Your Mind and They Will Take Your Soul

We live today in a spiritually sick society with every tradition undermined and every institution infiltrated by forces bent on destruction. It's right to reassess tradition in the light of contemporary consciousness but very foolish to do a 180-degree turnaround from it without fully understanding it, and we don't. We just denied the reality which tradition was trying to express. We could have changed the language somewhat but kept the meaning behind it or even gone more deeply into that meaning, but our intellectual pride was such that we failed to look beneath the surface of past ways of thinking.

As for national institutions, many of these had come to the point of decline which is why they could be captured and their functions subverted so easily. Once the process of infiltration had reached a certain stage there was a tipping point. That took place around the turn of the millennium after which time the mission became to carry through the new ideology rather than serve the interests the institution was set up for originally. Those who rose to the top in such circumstances were the ones who were most comfortable with the agenda or least hesitant to submit ambition to moral scruples. Inevitably, they employed and promoted like-minded people. Now, all institutions, both secular and spiritual, have been taken over and rededicated to different ideological ends. The appearance remains as a front, but the indwelling spirit has changed. It's a kind of possession.

The rejection of tradition and the destruction of institutions built up over, in some cases, centuries, did not happen by chance. It was not simply a matter of organic change but deliberate subversion. Every Western country was affected in the same way at the same time, and although it may seem as if this was simply how things turned out because of some fashionable -ism or the impact of the 1960s when class barriers tumbled and freedom and self-expression became the watchwords of the culture, that is not the case because these were only external manifestations of a spiritual revolution that was planned. When I use the word spiritual, I do not mean it was good. I mean it came from nonmaterial realms. It was part of a demonic attempt to corrupt humanity and separate it from God, to present evil as good and blacken spiritual good as evil. This could be done because elements of real good could be taken out of context, promoted, exaggerated, and used to deny others aspects of good. If you deny the primacy of the spiritual, then you can present material good as all that is required and what tends to spiritual good is dismissed as either irrelevant or even wicked because it conflicts with your material good.

The aim is control, both physical and psychological. One of the reasons the powers that be are trying to bring the era of cheap energy to a close is that they will have more control. Cheap energy gives freedom but when energy becomes expensive your individual freedom, certainly the power to exercise it, becomes much more circumscribed. Yet more important than this is control of thought. A tamed population does as it is told. This is why there has been this ongoing attempt to undermine men and masculinity. To emasculate is to control. It is why feminism and egalitarianism are pushed so relentlessly with the new sins of sexism and racism the worst thought crimes you can commit. It is true that the ideologies behind these supposed sins do have a core of validity, this being the value of the free individual, but the good in them has been deformed and made into an evil by being exaggerated and used to suppress other aspects of truth. A truth taken out of context and the area to which it applies and then applied to other areas in which it does not apply or not in the same way becomes a lie. But because there is a certain truth nestling within the two ideologies just mentioned it is hard to argue with them as they are presented now on an either/or basis which is what the argument usually gets reduced to. You must go above and beyond the good/bad dichotomy to find the truth about many things these days which is why we must go outside both conventional traditional and progressive thinking to get anywhere.

What is the aim of this undermining of freedom and attempted control of thought? For some in the outer circles it may be power but for the real instigators of the process it is the separation of Man from God. Spiritual not political. This is why there are so many contemporary movements that seek to rewrite the reality of creation. Dismantle creation and you do away with God to an even greater extent than simply not believing in him. As long as you accept the natural rules of creation you retain some link to its Maker, but when you no longer observe even these you have completely lost touch with reality. Then you can be moulded in whatever shape the demons who are behind all this wish. Give them your mind and they will take your soul.

A fundamental point to grasp about the end times is that they are the result of a process of decomposition. In old age the body breaks down and then it breaks up and is returned to the elements whence it arose, eventually to provide material for new life. This is what is taking place in the world today, and it is a natural part of the stage of the cycle in which we now live. That is one aspect of our current situation.

However, taking advantage of this process, riding on its back, as it were, are the dark forces which have the aim of separating human beings from their divine origins, partly to use them as energy sources since they can no longer receive energy directly from God so they must take it in a downgraded form, partly to make psychic slaves which can serve them, and partly because that is the nature of a being voided of light which is what they are and why their name is what it is. You have, therefore, this dual process in which natural decay is hurried along with deliberate stimulation and encouragement, and it applies to the psychological and spiritual realms even more than to the physical. Not true spiritual but spiritual as it is perceived and visualised in terms of the human mind.

Once you understand that our modern world is in a state of spiritual decay, much about it becomes clearer. Our material affluence is largely an inheritance from the past but also the result of focus on the material plane. It gives us the illusion of success, but it masks a yawning chasm of spiritual emptiness. Even liberalism, preposterous as this may sound to the mind indoctrinated with it, is the result of intellectual and moral decomposition, order dissolving into disorder and structure into chaos. That is not to say that conservatism of our day is any solution as that is mostly just a reaction against liberalism and not grounded, as it should be, in spiritual understanding.

There is no outer thing, group, institution, organisation, or even religion, in our world that can protect against the dissolving qualities of the end times. That is because they are all affected by those qualities. Some more than others but all are affected. Your only recourse is to go within and forge your own link to God, and that is what you are meant to do. You can certainly use outer things for support and guidance if you find that helpful, but you should do so with discrimination. You cannot rely on anything external to save you. I do not say you can save yourself, but you must go within to find that which can save you.

Celibacy

The act of sex is about making two into one on the horizontal plane while the spiritual path concerns making two into one on the vertical plane, and the analogy between these is not just metaphorical. In mysticism all souls are regarded as feminine to God, and the union between the soul and God is often described in terms of marriage.

Sex is fundamental to creation. Some people believe that the soul, as in our individual spiritual self, has no sex, being pure energy (whatever that means) with both masculine and feminine qualities held in balance, but the reality is that in any living being essence and existence are inseparable, which is to say that what you are and that you are, are two sides of the same coin. This means each soul is either masculine or feminine. The polarity of sex goes up to the highest level of creation, originating as we have noted in the division of spirit and matter, and as one ascends sex even becomes purer, less mixed. It is only on the very lowest levels of life, the nearest to base matter, that male and female blend into something like a unity in a lifeform. At the other extreme, unmanifest pure being may be beyond sexual division but in creation everything that is, is something and has either a masculine or feminine polarity. You can say this about North and South or Sky and Sea or Sun and Moon or even Time and Space. How much more can you say it about living beings?

Given there is a relation between sex and spirituality, it is necessary to understand the role sex might have or not have for one seeking to engage with the spiritual path on a serious level. In the past, celibacy was enjoined on those attempting to know God in many (not all) religions. Nowadays, it is not regarded as so essential though always the sexual energy is something to be controlled if one would transmute it to its higher counterpart on the spiritual plane.

The question then arises as to whether celibacy is part of the spiritual path and if it still has a place. First off, we should say that celibacy is not natural. Fruitfulness and fertility are wholesome expressions in the physical world of joy and creativity. Desire is godly because it is the flame of love as manifested in the human mind and body.

Yet while desire may be godly, attachment to desire is, if not sinful in itself, conducive to sin. It also binds one to the material world and material things. Now, celibates can be as full of desire as the promiscuous and sometimes even more so if suppressed energy, given no natural outlet, festers away beneath the surface and becomes a constant focus of attention, but the ideal of celibacy is to detach oneself from the world and be focused entirely on God. The world of matter, the Creation, is certainly good, but it is not the Creator, and it may be that to have a full relationship with God one must turn away from his things and face directly towards him. As far as we know, Jesus was celibate and he asked his disciples to devote themselves full time to their spiritual lives which is hard to do if you have a wife and children to support. This may be a requirement only for those who are seeking a deeper contact with God, but we may all have to become celibate at some time if we would attain to that deeper contact.

There are two aspects to the celibate life. One I have just mentioned, and that is the need to give proper attention to a wife and family. The married man cannot devote himself to God quite as much as the celibate. His attention is necessarily divided, at least until a certain later stage of married life. This goes for a woman too. That doesn't mean celibacy in itself is positive, but it may be a positive negative. The second aspect is sex itself. This mysterious energy is the most powerful we know of, excepting for some the love of God. While not being a need, it is more intense than any need and more fulfilling in its satisfaction. Some traditions speak of this energy requiring to be turned inwards and upwards rather than expressed outwardly, and would say that outward expression works against the reorientation inwardly just as a river cannot flow in two directions at the same time. We have to make water flow uphill, back to the source. A lot of spiritually interested people reject this idea nowadays, but it has a notable pedigree and one wonders if the modern rejection comes from the fact that we simply want to have our cake and eat it too, and look for reasons to justify doing what we want to do or are unable not to do.

Energy follows thought. In all cases, it is the mind that matters more than the body. By this criterion, actual celibacy is less important than the state of the mind. At the same time, a mind truly focused on God will naturally seek less external stimulation and result in a body requiring less external satisfaction.

In the ancient Indian way of spiritual development there were four stages of life known as *Asramas*. The first was that of the student known as *Brahmacharya* which lasted to about the age of 25 and in which celibacy was enjoined. Then came the stage of *Grihastha* which was that of the married householder wherein one raised a family and fulfilled and enjoyed all the material demands and satisfactions of life though always within a spiritual context meaning one of virtue and religious devotion. After the age of 50 came the retirement stage of *Vanaprastha* when one started to withdraw from the world and focus one's energies more on *Moksha,* liberation or salvation as we might call it in the West. If one wasn't celibate necessarily then sex was certainly something that should be receding from one's mind and attention. The fourth and final stage was that of *Sannyasa* which was the life of complete renunciation and here again celibacy was enjoined, though as the normal age for entering on this stage was 75, that should not be too much of a problem. This all represented the natural path of the soul through the world and returning to spirit, and I think still represents a good path for everyone though it should be noted that anyone could move into the *Sannyasa* stage straight from that of *Brahmacharya* if one felt particularly called to the spiritual life.

This Indian system tells us that celibacy has its place in the spiritual life, particularly at the beginning and end, but so does married life in which the full enjoyment of sex is not only permitted but encouraged as a good and healthy thing. There is no rejection of the body here but its incorporation into a grander scheme of things that has the aim of union with God, though for this to take place it is expected that the soul is able to move beyond the demands of the physical body, the energies of which must be purified and transmuted. This means desire must be directed towards God.

Some might think this Indian description of life stages has no relevance for the Christian, but I believe it has a universal application. If we think of the spiritual path as consisting of salvation and deification with the former as the preparatory stage and the latter as the ultimate aim, then we might say that celibacy has a role to play in the context of deification as a discipline and necessary condition for progress to be made. Every soul seeking full union with God, which union renders the soul divine, must develop an exclusive relationship with God and that means all other loves and attachments must be renounced. The creation must be renounced for full knowledge of the Creator. But this may just be a stage. If we say that God himself has a spouse which is the redeemed part of Creation (see the chapter Who Is Sophia?), every soul, as a reflection of its Creator, does likewise, and having reached conscious union with the Creator the soul can then turn back and re-embrace creation, though now in the full light of its divine identity.

Jesus said there was no marrying in heaven, but his first miracle was at a wedding and religion constantly speaks of spiritual completion in terms of a marriage. There might appear to be a contradiction here but perhaps Jesus was speaking in terms of earthly marriage. There is also spiritual marriage, eventually that between God and Creation but also for every individual soul, on the vertical plane with God its Creator and on the horizontal with its created other half. Celibacy relates to the union with God, but the sanctified soul does not just exist in that union. It also has relationships with other souls and among these is the reflection of the cosmic marriage of Spirit and Matter on its own level.

The significance of all this in relation to spiritual practice in the end times is that the waters become very muddied at this time with the encroachment of materialistic attitudes into the spiritual domain even where that exists. Purity and discipline are made to seem less important or relics from a less enlightened age when, in reality, to protect oneself from the corrupting influence of the present era, they are just as important as they ever were and maybe even more so in some respects. Everything crumbles in the end times, and sex is broken down to its base elements. In fact, sex lies at the heart of the Mysteries, but to understand that you have to see it in spiritual terms first and foremost. *Corruptio optimi pessima.*

Psychedelics and Religion

I am sympathetic to the people who advocate taking psychedelic drugs to enhance consciousness and explore inner realms. They would say this is especially beneficial in an atheistic society such as ours for it frees us from the iron grip of materialism and shines light into the dark clouds that obscure the modern mind. We are given the direct experience of something beyond standard physical plane consciousness, and we can know for ourselves that we are not body but mind, and that mind has multidimensional aspects. As a teenager I took LSD a few times so I know the transformative effect psychedelics can have, especially if you take them in a reverential frame of mind rather than for kicks, humbling yourself before the majesty of the universe and in an environment of outdoors natural beauty.

However, sympathy does not mean approval. I believe that the use of drugs, which is very ancient, came about when early human beings began to lose contact with the spiritual realms as the material world closed in about them. This was in line with the evolution of consciousness which requires the development of a solid centre, the self, and a rational thinking mind that can become a co-creator with God rather than a passive participant in the general spiritual flow of life. A lot of people try to get back to this flow but that is like a reversion to childhood, and it is spiritually immature. We must go forward into a new and higher awareness, one in which we do not merge into the all but become full spiritual individuals, mature, responsible, creative. Sometimes people need a cold shower rather than a warm bath to wake them up. Drugs were and are an escape. Early man resorted to them to try to recapture what he had lost but his spiritual progress demanded that he move on and did not revert to what he had known in the past.

Drugs are not recommended and never have been by any proper spiritual teacher. The reason is they are attempts to break the barrier God has placed between this world and the next by artificial means. This barrier can be broken but it should be broken by natural spiritual development if the encounter with the next world is to be authentic and psychically healthy. Drug takers may encounter nonmaterial beings in their experiences and these beings may seem to offer guidance and advice, but there are many denizens of the inner realms and you will not encounter true higher beings if you seek to take heaven by force. Your experience will be limited, and you may well only experience the world of the demons, albeit often dressed up to resemble what seems a deep and exciting mystery to the unwary.

We are not here to experience the glories of the spiritual world but to learn the lessons of the material one though with the understanding that the spiritual is primary. It is possible that in this benighted and ignorant age drugs can help guide one towards a previously dismissed and rejected higher reality but anything other than brief use will take you off the true spiritual path which is not about experience but the sanctification of the soul.

Since the Fall we have been cut off from Paradise. To attempt to recapture the paradisiacal state by artificial means, whether that be a drug or technique, special breathing, prolonged fasting or even excessive meditation, is an irreligious act that seeks to put you above God. The experience gained will be tainted and a counterfeit one to true mystical experience because it will be lacking the humility and purity of motive which alone guarantee truth and ascent to higher realms. It will lead the individual away from God as he really is and towards one of the many imitations that exist both in this world and the next. The fact that so many people who advocate psychedelics report encounters with pagan deities or similar supernatural beings confirms this. These, if not demons and they may well be, are leftovers from previous cycles of evolution. They continue to exist in the inner worlds but not on proper spiritual levels. They are forms that can be reanimated, after a fashion, by attention directed towards them, but the true spiritual life has departed from them.

Consciousness is a spiritual thing, but it is squeezed into a physical body to learn lessons which can eventually take it beyond the physical, and also beyond the spiritual as normally considered, to the divine. In a physical body consciousness becomes severely constricted but can also be focused, and express greater powers of self-will and motivation than when not limited in this way. To seek to escape this through drugs is to seek change from without, but for change to be real it must come from within. You reach the divine by becoming inwardly divine yourself not by attempting to steal what is not yours. A truly spiritual consciousness is not the result of what you experience or even what you feel or what you know. It comes from what you are, and for that to be of the right stuff demands humility, love of God, and openness to the spirit of Christ.

There are many people now who react against the materialism of contemporary culture and the shallowness of what religion has become, and seek to explore consciousness through psychedelic means, believing this will deepen their spiritual awareness and contacts. I'm afraid this simply shows the importance of discrimination and correct understanding of what the spiritual truly is. Spirituality is not higher consciousness. The devil has higher consciousness. It is orientation of the heart to goodness, beauty, and truth in their most elevated aspects together with a humble dedication to bring one's own soul into line with that regardless of what it may cost in terms of sacrifice and renunciation. And it will cost. If it doesn't, you're not doing it right. There is a tendency amongst educated (overeducated?) Westerners in our materialistic society to think that shamans in traditional cultures have a special insight which they lack because of the debilitating effects of civilisation and the perceived overemphasis on moral behaviour in Christianity which can become regimented and spiritually dry. This goes back at least as far as Rousseau's fantasies of the noble savage. But the shamans belonged to a previous cycle of evolution and what was right then is not now as consciousness has moved on. Some shamans may have powerful connections to plants and the intelligence behind plants, but this is not God for it relates to the inner workings of creation rather than to the Creator. It may be devas or nature spirits, it may be other discarnate intelligences, it may be demons, but fundamentally it is psychic rather than spiritual.

Westerners are certainly disconnected from that kind of world now, but they weren't always; witness our Neolithic cultures, something of which can still be sensed in the stone circles they left behind, but we moved away from that immersive state of consciousness in order to evolve. Going back to it is tempting for some who wish to escape the alienation of modern ego-consciousness but it is spiritually regressive and will not advance the soul because it indicates a refusal to grow and mature.

It may be that at one time plants and psychedelic substances were useful allies in the spiritual search but that time is long past. Today they are much more likely to open the mind up to malevolent forces from the psychic world that surrounds the physical one and give access to demons who will then influence consciousness, usually unbeknown to their victim. So much of the spiritual decadence that has come about since the 1960s can be laid at the door of the explosion of drug use that has taken place since then for when you open the door of the mind you are offering access to all sorts of nonmaterial beings, and those that dwell on higher levels will not come in that way. They cannot, for the spiritual only answers to the spiritual.

Is Equality a Spiritual Principle?

What is the goal of spirituality? What is its end point? Some would say it is the transcending of all limitations associated with the individual self and absorption into the universalized sea of consciousness in which the individual becomes one with the all, and time is swallowed up in eternity. For this no personal God is required. If he exists, then he too is ultimately part of the cosmic ocean. As we mentioned in an earlier chapter, the French writer Romain Rolland coined the term oceanic feeling to describe this experience which he seems to have become aware of through his study of the life of the 19th century Bengali mystic Ramakrishna who would frequently fall into spiritual raptures. The search for it is what lies behind many people's attraction to mysticism, especially of the Hindu and Buddhist variety.

We also referred to Freud's theory that the oceanic feeling is a reversion to a pre-ego state, something experienced by the infant before it becomes aware of self and other, and sees itself and its mother as one. The fact that Ramakrishna was an ardent devotee of the divine Mother, conceived by him as the goddess Kali, lends some incidental support to this theory.

Freud did not believe in the existence of the soul before birth and so he did not realise that the real roots of the oceanic feeling in which the sense of ego is blotted out is a reflection of the pre-incarnation state when the soul is not conscious of separation from its source, being still immersed in the pool of universal substance before being born into this dualistic world in which I and This are split apart. Thus, to experience the oceanic feeling may not be the indication of advanced spirituality it is sometimes taken to be. It *is* a spiritual experience but one pointing to the infancy of the soul prior to its exile. But the exile has a purpose (or else why bother with it?), and although we are destined to return to oneness it will not be the same oneness we left but a new version enriched with difference which enables full expression of all the glories of creation such as love, beauty, and goodness. There is no growth in primal oneness, no change, nothing but peace and bliss. It's a static condition, but our destined goal is not just to return to peace and bliss. Rather it is limitless expansion into light in which peace and bliss are invigorated by creative energy so that being and becoming combine to make something new.

What has all this to do with this chapter's title? If return to oneness really were the point of the spiritual path, then we could say that equality is a spiritual principle and one which we should be pursuing with vigour. The attempt to establish equality in the world would have the stamp of divine approval. But if this state of undivided oneness is a primordial condition signifying the world prior to creation that may not be so. An earlier chapter pointed out that the sea is the state of chaos or formlessness. In the beginning God divides the waters. Creation separates. It disrupts oneness and brings about differentiation. Now, you might say that, yes, it does do these things as it must if anything is to be, but we must return to the primordial state eventually because that is the ultimate reality.

The question then would be, in what way do we return? Do we do so in the same form we left and simply go back where we came from as if nothing had happened in the interim, or is there a point to creation? For what it all amounts to is, does God have a purpose in creating individual souls or not? Surely, we must assume he does or creation is meaningless. The journey through creation changes the souls making that journey. They are not intended to return to the spiritual cradle but to gain something they could not be given without earning for themselves. They are to become spiritual adults which means gods. They return to the source but in full consciousness of themselves as divine beings, and that means more individual not less. This is not an inevitable conclusion, and the soul may reject the opportunity but it is our destiny if we will take it. Those who do not may either be reabsorbed or else remain on one of the many levels of expressed being which exist between the gross material and the true divine.

I mention God having a purpose which carries the implication of God as a personal God. God as God the Father who loves us which, it is not generally appreciated, was a radically new idea when Jesus revealed it. Other spiritual approaches would present the highest spiritual reality as impersonal being which could not have a purpose. In that case to return to the state of pure oneness would be the path to pursue. But then this leaves so much not just unexplained but inexplicable. Why creation? Why love, why evolution? Why personhood in the first place, and how can the personal come from the non-personal? What is beauty and what is meaning if there is no person? No, the root of reality is personal not some kind of abstract nothing. This does not mean that God is a person as we are but that our personhood reflects his in a similar way as a line might be said to reflect a sphere in a more restricted dimensional mode. This is a clumsy analogy but it's the best I can do to make the point that God is a person, but that for him being a person is much more than it currently is for us.

Equality is not a spiritual principle. For anything to be, it must be something. One thing is never like another. Even blades of grass are different, and the more a thing develops, the more it unfolds of its divine nature, the more individual it becomes. True equality is found in one place only and that is in the realm of non-manifestation. Equality directly contradicts individuality, which is a spiritual principle, one grounded in freedom, freedom being the fundamental spiritual quality and impossible in a purely material world. Inequality is only a problem when it is used as an excuse for the strong to dominate the weak, but then that is a corruption and sin against love, and no reason to try to enforce equality any more than the possibility of hate might lead one to suppress love.

"I saw a new heaven and a new earth, for the first heaven and the first earth had passed away, and there was no more sea." I return to this passage from the Book of Revelation. We are looking here at the end of time when all things are completed and the earthly creation has run its course. Everything has been brought to fulfilment and the unrefined raw material of pure consciousness represented by the sea has been transformed into the glorious company of saints, the inhabitants of the New Jerusalem. The sea is that from which life emerges. In its primordial form it is the one place there might be said to be equality, and so we can define egalitarianism as the desire to return to the pre-created state where there is no distinction. It is not the mark of proper spiritual understanding for that sees every individual soul as unique which, by definition, means different and therefore not equal.

The goal of establishing equality can either be regarded as well-meaning and motivated by a desire for fairness, or else as an attempt to impose conformity on a populace to make it more controllable and separate it from higher aspects of reality. In fact, the former group can be used by the latter to bring about a society in which all the mountaintops have been levelled and eventually nobody even believes in mountains. This should make it obvious that egalitarianism is not so much socially progressive as spiritually reductive. Could the drive towards equality turn out to be a means of enforcing spiritual slavery?

St. Michael

If you were looking for a patron saint to whom you could turn for guidance and protection in the end times you could hardly do better than St. Michael the Archangel. The nature of these times does not just call for contemplatives. It needs warriors for truth too who will speak out against the lies of materialism, atheism, and false ideologies of all kinds, including false spiritual ideologies. Now is a time when the image of St. Michael crushing Satan should be at the forefront of anyone's mind who is concerned with defending goodness and truth.

St. Michael is the captain of the army of God, the leader of the heavenly hosts. Why would God have an army? Isn't he all to do with peace and love, and doesn't he teach turning the other cheek and not resisting evil? All that is quite true. The basic task of the Christian is to fight evil in his own soul. We are told to forgive those who trespass against us, both for their sake and for our own because holding a grudge damages the soul, causing a dark stain which deepens and spreads if not wiped clean by forgiveness. That is why we are advised to repay hatred with love. But this is on the personal level, in relation to what is done to us. We are also called to fight evil in the world provided our motivation for doing so is love of God not personal. We are not told to accept or tolerate evil, or to ignore it when it is out there in the world. In that case we must combat it for if we fail to do so it will grow and triumph. The injunction not to resist evil does not mean you should not fight it. You absolutely should but with a heart free of hatred for those who have allowed themselves to be the vessels for it. Christ is called the Prince of Peace, and he promised his disciples a peace beyond that of this world, but he also said he did not come to bring peace but a sword. You reconcile these apparent contradictions by seeing there can be no peace with evil out there but there is a higher peace, a more positive thing that is not mere absence of conflict, which comes from conquering the evil in our own hearts. Inspired by the reality of this peace we can go to war against evil.

If Aragorn and Gandalf had not fought against Sauron, then Sauron would have taken over the world and turned it into a wasteland. *The Lord of the Rings* is a spiritual document of a high order, and these two men are expressions of the warrior and priest archetypes respectively. They serve in the lineage of St. Michael and Christ, and just as Christ incarnates the Love of God so St. Michael represents God's Will. Consequently, he is associated with the element of fire. God is certainly Love but he also has a sword, and it is wielded by St. Michael. That is not to say everyone should take up arms as Tolkien's heroes did, but the principle of mental fight is the same.

There are many places in the world where St. Michael is celebrated but the abbey at Le Mont-Saint-Michel in Normandy may be his most important sanctuary. It is certainly the most striking in terms of its setting as well as the most visited. Here is a little history.

In the year 708 AD the Archangel Michael appeared in a dream to Bishop Aubert of Avranches, a town in the southwest of Normandy, and told him to build a church on a rocky island that lay in the large bay at the mouth of the river Couesnon a few miles away. The bishop doubted the veracity of his dream and St. Michael had to return on two further occasions to convince him of the truth of the vision. Even then, the only way the archangel could do this was by pressing his finger so strongly into the bishop's head that he left a round hole there. The poor man's skull, complete with hole, still exists for all to see in the Saint-Gervais Basilica in Avranches.

Anyway, this rather extreme measure worked, and the church was built. In the 11th century a Romanesque abbey was constructed with Gothic style refectory and cloisters added 200 years later. Further buildings were completed in the ensuing centuries, and finally in 1895 a statue of St. Michael himself, dragon underfoot, was put at the top of the spire, giving it its current appearance. At the time of the French Revolution the island and its buildings were converted into a prison which is symbolically apt, but that was closed in 1863. Monks began to return in the 20th century, and now there is a small community of monks and nuns living there and continuing the over 1000-year-old tradition of prayer and worship.

Whether by accident or design, Le Mont-Saint-Michel is a microcosm of the medieval world or ideal Christian society. At the top there stands Saint Michael, representing God and protecting the monastery founded in his name. Below him there is the Benedictine abbey where monks lived their lives in worship and prayer. Descending a little further are the halls for noble guests (the aristocracy), and below them the shops and houses of the tradespeople who represent the everyday world. Outside the walls there were some rough dwellings for those who did the menial work required to keep such a place running. Even today when you visit the Mount, as around three million people do every year, you have the feeling of ascending through worldly levels towards God. When you enter the large gate after traversing a causeway that runs from the mainland there is a 15th century English cannon captured during the 100 Years War. Perhaps an appropriate symbol for a site dedicated to the Warrior of God. You join a noisy, bustling crowd going in and out of shops selling tourist knickknacks or visiting one of the Mount's several restaurants. Then as you climb the winding path that leads to the top the crowd seems to thin out. The ascent becomes a little more difficult, the steps steeper, until eventually you leave the commercial world behind and stand in front of the abbey doors. Entering the abbey, you carry on climbing until you reach a large platform outside the main church from where there is a magnificent view of the bay. Then you enter the church and are in a completely different space in which the mundane is left behind and the sacred is all around you. It is peaceful and the vaulted columns of the choir lift your spirits heavenwards.

St. Michael fighting the dragon above Le Mont-Saint-Michel.
From Les Très Riches Heures du Duc de Berry

Here are some of the titles that St. Michael is regarded as holding. The first is a translation of his name, and should be read as a question.

1. Who is like God.
2. Recorder of the deeds of men in the Heavenly Books.
3. The Celestial Medium through whom the Law was given.
4. Captain of the Heavenly Hosts.
5. Slayer of the dragon of evil intention.
6. Guardian of the Holy Sanctuaries.
7. Preparer of the Way before each Messenger from God.
8. Leader of the Church Triumphant in Heaven and Militant on Earth.

These are all Christian titles and relate to the war in heaven described in Revelation 12:7–10 where Michael fights against the great dragon who is Satan, overcomes him and casts him down to the earth. But does he appear in other places too? There are solid grounds for thinking he does because figures analogous to Michael exist in many ancient myths which recount how a hero or god overcomes a monstrous dragon. To name a few, India has the story of Indra who kills the serpent Vritra as related in the Rig Veda. Greek myth has Zeus battling the dragon Typhon, as well as Apollo who kills the great snake Python in order to set up his oracle at Delphi. In the Babylonian epic of creation, the storm god Marduk slays Tiamat who is described as a sea serpent. All of these are solar or sky deities who overcome chthonic powers represented by the serpent or dragon. The Indra, Zeus, and Marduk stories have been interpreted as symbolising cometary impacts at the end of the last Ice Age, but they also could be mythical descriptions of the attempt by the developing human ego to separate itself from the power of instinctual nature which is why the serpent is often conceived of as female. The non-Christian legends are a little different to the legend of St. Michael as these ancient monsters are more primeval than evil, but still something of the same process may be identified as it may in the stories of heroes such as St. George, Sigurd, and Beowulf.

The old legends are interesting in that they tell us something about previous cycles of evolution, whether you interpret that as cometary bombardment of the Earth, the struggle by early humanity to establish a free and self-determining consciousness, or simply to describe the battle against evil. Or even all three. But what of St. Michael now? He is clearly a solar being whose mission it is to bring light to darkness which he does both in terms of shining a light into unevolved consciousness and fighting against the dark forces that threaten to overturn proper spiritual development. In terms of his mission in the end times, it is primarily the second of these two roles that is important, as captured in the picture above. Spiritual evil is rampant in the end times, and it must be actively combatted.

In 1884 Pope Leo XIII was reported to have had a vision in which he heard a conversation between the Devil and Jesus Christ. During this conversation the Devil threatened to destroy the Catholic Church over the next century. He asked for a greater influence over those who would give themselves to his service and this was granted by Christ, presumably as a test for the faithful. The Pope was so shaken by what he heard in that vision that he straightaway composed a prayer to St. Michael, imploring his protection against "that ancient serpent who is called the devil." Coincidentally or not, it was also around this time that Rudolf Steiner claimed that St. Michael entered into greater proximity to the Earth as part of his mission to progress human evolution. We can accept these two accounts at face value or not, but it is striking that two men from different spiritual backgrounds and with different approaches, Catholic and esoteric, had a similar vision at the same time, even if each expressed it in his own language and according to his own understanding. It lends support to the idea that the spiritual power known as St. Michael has been called forth once again to deal with the reappearance of the dragon in our times. Given the trajectory of the world over the last century one might wonder how successful he has been, but the nature of the end times cannot be avoided so it may be that St. Michael can only help those who actively seek his support. According to Pope Leo, evil has been given its head and the natural currents of life are with it in the present age, but those who see it and wish to resist it will be given aid and protection.

Christians and the Esoteric

It is said that there is nothing esoteric in Christianity. Everything is public and out in the open, and there are no hidden secrets divulged only to higher level initiates. And it is true that Christ did exteriorise the mysteries, enacting literally what had taken place symbolically in those ancient rites and so potentially making rebirth into spirit available to everyone who believed in him, though what belief in Christ really means in this context is something to ponder. But time moves on and what was applicable at one moment in history may be less so later.

Spirituality means escaping the iron grip of matter. Not because matter is evil but because it is matter, i.e. not spirit or not spirit in its pristine, undisguised form. As one escapes matter one moves up through the levels of manifested reality which, in human terms, means through the levels of the physical nature, the emotions, thought, and personal identity. Each one of these levels must be conquered but all are incorporated into the whole. We descend from the pure consciousness of the spiritual world into matter to learn the lessons of matter and acquire its virtues which are the qualities associated with action and doing, relating and feeling, and knowing and understanding, qualities one can only acquire through experience in a world of duality. In the process of our immersion in matter we forget who we are and identify with the 'bodies' or modes of being through which we temporarily operate in order to gain the ability to become gods, free agents with creative power motivated by love. It is this false identification that is the problem, so the fault does not lie with matter, which is merely the medium through which spirit expresses and comes to know itself, but our identification with it.

What does this have to do with the esoteric? Simply this. At an earlier phase of development, most human beings were focused on the physical and emotional worlds. Few had developed mentally to a high level, but that is no longer the case. Many people have now reached a relatively high degree of intellectual development, and these people need to understand. They cannot just proceed on faith. Their ability to believe must be coupled with understanding for them to flourish and grow spiritually, and for their belief to be rooted in the whole of their being. The esoteric is about knowledge. It is not spiritual in the spiritual sense but intellectual. And yet for modern man to be spiritual in the spiritual sense he needs intellectual support.

A follower of Christ in our day must combine a degree of esoteric understanding with faith. If he neglects this his faith will be shallow even if it is intense. His spiritual development will be limited and his entry into the mind of Christ will be partial. This is in line with the growth of human consciousness. The old ways may suffice for some but, for those who would not just follow Christ but start to become like him, knowledge must supplement faith even if it remains the case that true understanding arises from real faith. *"Credo ut intelligam,"* in the words of St. Anselm, the 11th century Archbishop of Canterbury.

The esoteric is not there to replace faith in Christ. It is not a higher level of spirituality but a means of deepening faith and elevating it to a plane where the boundaries between feeling and knowing start to disappear. If faith is of the heart, then the esoteric is of the head and we need both to be spiritually complete. Indeed, only when we have both do we really have either one of them in the proper sense.

All that is hidden will be revealed. This is one of the advantages of living in the end times. We have been given access to so much that was secret, partly because that is the nature of the times but also because enough of us are now capable of deriving more benefit than harm from the revealed knowledge. But it would be a mistake because of this to write off Christianity as belonging to the past. Over the last 150 years with the release of esoteric knowledge people have looked in many places for spiritual enlightenment, often adopting various forms of what has become known as New Age spirituality which was regarded as a more advanced form of religious understanding with greater insights than conventional approaches. It is true that the official channels of Christianity have fallen away from the purity of truth as they have become infected by secularism, but the fact remains that the real New Age religion is Christianity, and we only fail to recognise this because we are so used to it. Read the Gospels, particularly that of St. John, and you will see why this is so. Christ brought something entirely new to the world which was the chance of entrance to a new creation in which the material or outer was made fully transparent to the spiritual or inner. He made possible the union of Heaven and Earth, and this was expressed symbolically by the New Jerusalem, a city built by God but with the aid of man, all of whose selfless deeds, noble thoughts, and truly creative acts go into the construction. The fact that in the Christian mythos the original garden of Eden becomes the heavenly city of Jerusalem shows we are not just returning to the paradisiacal perfection of eternity but, through time, forging something new. No other religion or spiritual path has this vision.

The New Age religions of the 20th century were mostly jumbles of ancient beliefs mashed up together and presented as new. They included bits of ancient paganism with a smattering of Eastern mysticism, a touch of occultism, and a seasoning of psychically received messages from the inner planes, some worthwhile, many not, but little of this was new as such. It did point to the immanence of God which was a good corrective to the conventional Christian idea of God as largely transcendent, but it was also heavily influenced by what you might call the

Babylonian Mystery religion which is one of the oldest false paths around, going right back to the Fall of Man and the attempt to become a god independently of God. New Age religion was not demonic in itself, but it had the potential to become so because it was more focused on gaining experience in the psychic and spiritual worlds than on sanctifying the soul. The demons can give mystical highs or the semblance of them, but they cannot convey the sense of the holy, and it is holiness not spirituality that opens the door to the real New Age when Man will enter into full communion with God and work with him in the glorification of the universe.

Don't Worry, This Was Inevitable

It's hard to watch the civilisation of which you are a part destroy itself, especially when that civilisation has created many great and noble things in the past and reached heights that earlier civilisations had not attained both in terms of art and science and religious sophistication. And it's perplexing that so many people don't see this though I suspect that more are beginning to do so as the suicidal nature of our civilisation becomes increasingly evident and its behaviour ever more absurd.

It's also strange that so many members of that civilisation seem hellbent on dragging it down into the mire. We talk of envy and resentment, and these are obviously major drivers in this scenario, but are they sufficient to explain the sheer lunacy of much present-day behaviour? I don't think they are. Large numbers of people in the modern age suffer from a profound spiritual disorder and one can only speculate what has caused this. Is it the self-hatred of the decadent? Is it the rebellion against God of the proud? Or is it due to an infirmity of the soul which the demonic forces can capture and use? I have mentioned previously that in the end times all the flotsam and jetsam of the past age rises to the surface and, while we may be reluctant to admit it, that is true in human terms as well. Spiritual rebels and laggards are being given a chance to make good if they will but take it.

Everything is degrading, even if the worsening is obscured for the time being by our relative prosperity for people can put up with a lot with a full stomach, but it is important we do not succumb to despair. The best way to avoid this is to realise that nothing lasts in this world. Everything goes through a spring, summer, autumn, and winter cycle. This is how things are in a world in which decay or entropy is the backdrop to everything as it must be in a material world since only spirit endures. We are now in deep midwinter. Then we must realise that the West had the defects of its qualities. For a while the latter dominated but now the former have emerged and are bringing the whole thing down. Our civilisation contained the seeds of its own destruction, and these have now sprouted so that the weeds are choking the flowers. The main quality of the West was the strong sense of an individual self and the concomitant idea of freedom. This has made our civilisation. But its downside is the egotism and, more especially, the tendency of self to remove God from his throne and install itself there. This is what we have done both collectively and individually. The idea that we can remake creation in our own image is a consequence of that. The West also birthed the machine through its exploration of natural science. This had the benefits we know but it was also a Frankenstein's monster that has certainly turned against us. Materially miraculous but spiritually deadly. Would we have been better off without it? That's the wrong way to look at the situation. The advent of the machine had to be as all possibilities must work themselves out at the end of an age which is where we currently are. We could have reacted better to it but the descent of consciousness into matter made it inevitable in some form.

The second bulwark against any despair that might arise as our world crumbles is to realise that our true home is not here but Heaven. This life is a learning experience. We are only visitors, and the world is meant as a bridge not a home. If we are alive at this time, it is because we are meant to be alive now. There are lessons we can learn, and services we can render. We should value the past and try to preserve what is good in it, but we cannot preserve it forever because all things pass. And yet, nothing truly good can ever be lost, and whatever is good here is but a reflection of a reality elsewhere. Perfection does exist but it is not in this world which exists just to make us worthy of perfection. The material civilisation of the West is passing but all the good in it will be taken up and go into the construction of the New Jerusalem.

This does not mean we should not try to make this world as true a reflection of the higher worlds as it can be. All great civilisations of the past have done just that which is what makes them great civilisations and makes it easier for members of those civilisations to coordinate themselves to spiritual reality. But when worldly conditions make that impossible, we must accept the inevitable with detachment. There are spiritual lessons to be learned at such a time that cannot be learned in better times because there is not the challenge to bring them forth.

This, then, is the task for the present-day spiritual disciple. Seek always to manifest and uphold the good and the true but know that, as far as the wider world is concerned, your efforts will be largely in vain. It doesn't matter. It's not your responsibility. Your responsibility is to God and your own soul, and then to any other souls whom God may send in your direction. In other words, love God and love your neighbour. The best way you can help the wider world is by doing this because you are shining a light in darkness, which light will spread and be picked up by others in ways you cannot know.

Many people get discouraged because their efforts bring forth no obvious results. That is especially so in our day because something of the celebrity culture mindset (another sign, incidentally, of decadent times) rubs off even on those on the spiritual path. They think outer success is a mark of spiritual achievement. That is to judge the spiritual by the standards of the worldly. In the great majority of cases the results of your endeavours will only become apparent after you have left this world. Part of the test of a true disciple is that he perseveres even when there is no sign of him getting anywhere, and this is even more the case in the end times when everything in your favour is against you as a friend of mine used to say.

The abandonment by the West of Christianity meant it no longer had a properly working immune system, and left it open to infection by viruses from outside and by decay from within which it could no longer counter. If it is not already dead, it is certainly dying. The only recourse for the spiritual man at such a time is to accept the inevitable. The descent cannot be arrested nor reversed. It must proceed to its due end. All you can do is detach yourself from identification with the process and attend to your own soul, making it right with God. When Jesus came, he did seek to establish an earthly kingdom but taught us to love and serve God and set our hearts on the Kingdom of Heaven. This teaching still stands. The world will not change its path because that is the nature of the end times. You should certainly stand up for the Truth but with the knowledge that at this time there is no worldly victory. Victory there will be, but it is not here.

Conclusion

This book is about the end times and how we may best respond to them so that we are not swept along by the materialistic forces that dominate then. But, as we have noted, many traditions describe these times as the conclusion of a grand cycle in which the environment, both physical and psychic, deteriorates so, although it is outside the main scope of this book, it is worth briefly considering what might be responsible for this cycle and cause the changes both we as human beings and the Earth itself experience during the course of it. These changes involve an initial rarefied state and then progressive degradation of the atmosphere as the cycle continues over the thousands of years it exists. It is said the actual structure of matter undergoes alteration over that time, becoming denser and therefore increasingly impermeable to spiritual impulse, and consciousness changes in line with that. Esoteric theory does, in fact, state that there has been a densification of matter over the ages as the Earth takes full physical form, resulting in our present hard and solid condition, and, while it's unlikely the timescales match, this, in part, might account for the spiritual loss suffered in the descent from the Gold to Iron Ages. Other ideas range from simple entropic decay as we move further away from an initiating first times when spiritual energy is introduced into the system, basically old age, to some kind of influence from the cosmos experienced by our planet as it travels through space. This latter is a purely mechanistic explanation and should not obscure the underlying reality that behind it there would be spiritual purpose for which it is simply the agent. Mind lies behind everything. Also, none of these ideas take into account the factor of the Incarnation which adds something significantly new to the mix. Christ does not annul the cyclical order of the ages but brings some linearity and focus to it. Before and after Christ are radically different times which is why the end times are like but also different to the Kali Yuga.

Having said all this, I should emphasise that what matters is understanding the nature of the end times, and, most of all, our spiritual response to them. Their cause, whether it be the result of entropy or ongoing densification of matter as part of our planet's descent from a more rarefied form or a change in the cosmic ecosystem we traverse, or even a combination of all of these, is not so important. We should also be clear that just as the stars incline but do not compel, so the degraded environment of the end times does not justify us capitulating to it. We have the truth within us in all its purity so should not succumb to external conditions, whatever they may be.

It is said that in the Satya Yuga or Golden Age there was no caste. This does not mean there was equality as we understand the term nowadays, but that in those prelapsarian days only souls of a certain spiritual level and similar status incarnated, in consequence of which there was universal harmony. Now, in the Kali Yuga, it is a spiritual free for all with all manner of different souls from different backgrounds appearing on the Earth, which is one of the reasons for disagreements and war, though, on the plus side, surmounting these obstacles does have the potential to bring about inner growth. But the caste structure was originally required in the Kali Yuga to provide a framework for harmony as harmony does not come naturally under the conditions of that time, especially as there is such a wide variety of souls. One might regard the recent dismantling of caste as an attempt to build a new Golden Age were it not for the fact that the nature of these times plus that variety make such an eventuality impossible. It's better to live according to the rules of your own age rather than those of another even if those other rules seem superior from a more universal point of view. They are still less appropriate for the age in which you live because the spiritual quality of that age is fundamentally different. The fact that our rules are breaking down is more likely to indicate that we are at the tail end of the Kali Yuga when even its norms fall apart than building a new Golden Age from the material available to us here and now. And if that is the case, we must ask the question, what comes next?

Reconciling the cyclical scheme of the Indian Yugas with the linear Christian view of time is not easy. There is obvious overlap between the two, but they are not the same though I have treated them as similar here because it is clear they are expressing a similar truth in the context of their different spiritual outlooks. The most important similarity is that between the nature of the end times and the Kali Yuga, which both represent major spiritual loss and the triumph of materialism and are followed by the reappearance of a divine figure, Christ or the Kalki avatar. As this book is about the end times and how best to negotiate them it makes sense to look at the present age in the light of both Indian and Christian predictions, but what happens after that? There seems to be some disagreement on the Indian side as to whether the Kali Yuga concludes with the restoration of the Golden Age after the incarnation of the divine avatar who rights all wrongs, or whether after the Kali Yuga there is a return to the Satya Yuga, but only after traversing the Dwapara (Bronze) and Treta (Silver) Yugas. In other words, do you go straight to the top from the bottom and then descend or do you ascend to the top gradually before descending again? Since in both cases there are prolonged transitionary periods between the ages which involve geological upheaval and mass destruction, possibly caused by cometary impact, there is a wiping clean of the slate before entering the new age so it doesn't make much difference to most of us what that new age might be, living, as we are, at the end of the Kali Yuga. There will be a new population then even though it will have been seeded from the old.

The Christian scheme is linear, i.e. historical. There is a goal which there does not appear to be in the Yuga system. I believe there is truth in both stories. The pagan accounts (Indian, Greek, and others) relate the cyclical process that prevailed before the incarnation of Christ. The Christian account disrupts the traditional cycle by giving the journey a purpose and making it go somewhere. In that sense, the order of the Yuga cycle is disturbed by a significant new factor. Nevertheless, for the immediate future both traditions are in agreement. That from India predicts we will shortly be entering a transition period between one age and the next which will entail the widespread breakdown of global society, and environmental breakdown as well. And in Christianity, the end times, which equates more to the end of the Kali Yuga than the whole period, the very last phase of the cycle, brings similar bad news with wars, famines, and earthquakes on the agenda. The Book of Revelation predicts the sun turning black, the moon becoming blood red in appearance, and the stars falling to earth which might be describing cometary bombardment and a shift in the polar axis, a scenario supported by other sources. The difference is that the one says we will subsequently enter a new phase of an ongoing cycle while the other anticipates the return of Christ which does not just initiate a new age but brings a new creation in which there is no more death.

A new phase in the cycle or a new creation, which is it? These could be different, culturally specific, ways of describing the same thing, and I am going to say that this difference is not of primary importance for those of us alive today anyway as our immediate future is the end times collapse. And I would add that whatever takes place in that collapse, death and destruction included, does not matter so much because it relates to circumstances in this world, and we are told to be in the world but not of it. Our goal is the heavenly world and that is where we should be focusing our attention. Let this world do what it will. If destruction comes and the stars fall to the earth, so be it. We all die at some point anyway. This is not our true home so what happens here should not concern us overmuch. Which is not to say we don't care, but we don't care unduly. This is the end times, but those times only affect this world, and we are merely sojourners here. If you would survive the forthcoming collapse in the only way that matters, then know that you come from elsewhere and will shortly be returning there. Just make sure before you return that you have done what you came here to do in the sense of learning lessons that are only possible at such a time of spiritual breakdown.

The world may be entering a new era of spiritual understanding, but it will require a thorough and complete cleansing first, and that is the imminent next stage. Our task is to purify ourselves so that whatever comes to pass we are properly prepared. When all is said and done, surviving the end times means becoming a saint or, at least, setting one's foot on the path to sainthood. That is the purpose and goal of the whole process of earthly life.

About the Author

William Wildblood was born in London. After a period working as an antiques dealer, he left the UK to run a guesthouse in South India. He later moved to France where he was an occasional guide at the medieval abbey of Le Mont-Saint-Michel. He returned to England at the end of the twentieth century, working for various magazines including seven years as an antiques columnist. He has written several other books including *Meeting the Masters, Remember the Creator, Earth is a School,* and *By No Means Equal. The Spiritual Crisis of Modern Man* is a collection of his online writings, and he also contributed to *Albion Awakening* with John Fitzgerald.

MANTRA
BOOKS

EASTERN RELIGION & PHILOSOPHY

We publish books on Eastern religions and philosophies. Books that aim to inform and explore the various traditions that began in the East and have migrated West.

If you have enjoyed this book, why not tell other readers by posting a review on your preferred book site.

Recent Bestsellers from MANTRA BOOKS Are:

The Way Things Are

A Living Approach to Buddhism

Lama Ole Nydahl

An introduction to the teachings of the Buddha, and how to make use of these teachings in everyday life.

Paperback: 978-1-84694-042-2 ebook: 978-1-78099-845-9

Back to the Truth

5000 Years of Advaita

Dennis Waite

A demystifying guide to Advaita for both those new to, and those
familiar with this ancient, non-dualist philosophy from India.

Paperback: 978-1-90504-761-1 ebook: 978-184694-624-0

Shinto: A Celebration of Life

Aidan Rankin

Introducing a gentle but powerful spiritual pathway reconnecting
humanity with Great Nature and arming all aspects of life.

Paperback: 978-1-84694-438-3 ebook: 978-1-84694-738-4

In the Light of Meditation

Mike George

A comprehensive introduction to the practice of meditation and the spiritual principles behind it. A 10 lesson meditation programme with CD and internet support.

Paperback: 978-1-90381-661-5

The 7 Levels of Wisdom

Mónica Esgueva

A straightforward and compelling approach on how to reach the highest levels of consciousness, wisdom, and inner peace.

Paperback: 978-1-80341-470-6 ebook: 978-1-80341-471-3

Compassion Based Living Course

Heather Regan-Addis and Choden

A practical guide to living a compassionate life.

Paperback: 978-1-80341-676-2 ebook: 978-1-80341-709-7

The Sacred Gathas of Zarathushtra & the Old Avestan Canon

Pablo Vazquez

The ancient and mystical poetry of Zarathushtra and the first Zoroastrians: Now accessible to the public in a modern translation.

Paperback: 978-1-78535-961-3 ebook: 978-1-78535-962-0

Radiant Bliss

Sue Bushell

Embrace Your Journey: Unfolding Peace, Power, and Purpose Through Yoga

Paperback: 978-1-80341-818-6 ebook: 978-1-80341-822-3

Ordinary Women, Extraordinary Wisdom

Rita Marie Robinson

The Feminine Face of Awakening

A collection of intimate conversations with female spiritual teachers who live like ordinary women, but are engaged with their true natures.

Paperback: 978-1-84694-068-2 ebook: 978-1-78099-908-1

The Riddle of Alchemy

Paul Kiritsis

What is alchemy, exactly? Is there any empirical truth to ancient speculative pursuits toward metallic transmutation? How does alchemy intersect with Western mind sciences and science in general?

Paperback: 978-1-80341-637-3 ebook: 978-1-80341-688-5

Readers of ebooks can buy or view any of these bestsellers by clicking on the live link in the title. Most titles are published in paperback and as an ebook. Paperbacks are available in traditional bookshops. Both print and ebook formats are available online.

Find more titles and sign up to our readers' newsletter at www.collectiveinkbooks.com/mind-body-spirit. Follow us on Facebook at facebook.com/OBooks and Twitter at twitter.com/obooks